Isabel Bishop in her Studio/Photo by Walter Daran

Isabel Bishop

Published by
The University of Arizona Museum of Art
Tucson, Arizona
1974

The First Retrospective Exhibition held in American Museums
of Paintings, Drawings, Etchings and Aquatints by Isabel Bishop

Limited Edition
2500 Printed

Contents

Foreword

Many things have been said about Isabel Bishop which are true, so far as they go, but fail to reach what I think is the central quality of her art. Much has been made of her fascination with Union Square and the variety of human beings who inhabit it. Her impeccable draughtsmanship, her sensitive handling of light, her uncanny awareness of the moment at which an action must be frozen to imply the motions surrounding it have all been noted with eminent justice. They are important elements in her work.

But beyond them lies a quality hard to define which can perhaps be suggested by words like stillness, monumentality and tradition. Her figures are there, they exist, they have that living reality which one feels in a Rembrandt portrait or a Rubens nude. They do not look like Rembrandt or Rubens—they are not eclectic—but in some mysterious manner which I do not really understand they carry forward the great tradition of North-European, seventeenth-century figure painting.

Cézanne once said his aim was to make Impressionism as solid and durable as the art of museums. In her own way, Isabel Bishop has sought and found a comparable solidity with a comparable independence of means. Her people have a moving, inward quality, although that may be a subjective response on my part. Beyond argument is their monumental existence—in terms of both humanity and art.

John I. H. Baur

Introduction

As the father of three young daughters, I am concerned with the limited accomplishments women have been able to make in the arts, particularly the visual arts. So many American women have embarked upon careers as painters or sculptors, yet so few have succeeded. In literature, on the other hand, numerous women have been outstanding. The names of Willa Cather, Edna St. Vincent Millay, Pearl Buck, Margaret Mitchell, Katherine Anne Porter, and Joyce Carol Oates immediately come to mind; but in the art world only a handful have achieved a similar recognition.

Isabel Bishop is one of those rare exceptions. Shortly before World War I she left Detroit to settle in New York's Union Square, a most improbable area for a young woman from the Midwest, and set out to become an artist at a time when her chances of success were slim indeed. In spite of the obstacles that confronted her, she quickly gained the admiration and affection of colleagues and critics alike. She never felt deprived because she was a woman, nor did she feel discriminated against. And she discovered that getting along in a male-dominated art world was less formidable than one might imagine, even in an era when women were expected to marry, remain at home, and raise children. This is why Isabel Bishop impresses me as being a very special woman.

Although an artist's life may appear quite romantic to those who live far from the streets of New York, the illusion is quickly dispelled by the grim realities of life in a crowded and impersonal city. Isabel Bishop had to strive simply to keep her body and soul together in those early years; more often than not, it proved to be a daily task. Marriage was unthinkable. She had to work hard merely to exist in a world where youthful aspirations were frequently subjected to harsh criticism and sometimes cruel ridicule. But she fought to make a place for herself and, in doing so, she gained the respect of her teachers, Guy Pène du Bois and Kenneth Hayes Miller, and also won the regard of two fellow artists, Reginald Marsh and Edwin Dickinson. They worked and lived on nearby 14th Street.

"We would meet for lunch or dinner to discuss our day's work," she fondly recalls. "By tradition each of us paid for our own fifty cent meal." Occasionally Marsh would take her to a Coney Island dance marathon or backstage at Minsky's Burlesque. "It was great going with Reggie," she says. "Reg drew, but I just wasn't up to it, and once in a while Minsky even bought Reggie's work."

By this time Isabel had begun to find herself as an artist and liked to visit Union Square where she would draw for hours. "I adored it," she remembers. "Drawing nourished my spirit; it was like eating. I got ideas there, for drawing is a way of finding out something, even though it might only be the discovery of a simple gesture." If the idea were good, she would test it on an etching plate, then perhaps paint it. After a while she came to feel right at home in the Square. One day she decided, rather apprehensively, to approach a strange man and ask if she could draw him in her studio. "Want me to take my clothes off?" he inquired with an impish smile. He did pose with his clothes on, however, and proved to be even more frightened than Isabel herself.

Many of the Square's inhabitants served as models for her paintings in the years that followed; later some of her "models" would sit around the large statue of George Washington on his horse and laugh about it. Sometimes they were drunk, but even then she was fascinated by them. "They were so beautiful. What marvelous configurations their bodies had ... and, oh, those rumpled clothes." "If you want us," they would say, "we'll be under the horse's tail."

Once, while sketching in the Square, a drunk annoyed her. Isabel bristled in her most elegant manner in an attempt to discourage him. But her response was a mistake. The man, feeling as though he had been used by this "rich lady," hailed his cohorts. A small and resentful mob soon demanded that she give up her sketch book. Instead, she tore off a single page, handed it to one of the men, and slowly moved toward a policeman who was standing at the edge of the park. Much to her horror the policeman sided with the bums. In his opinion, she had invaded their domain. "I felt hurt," she said, "as though my home had turned on me, but later on I realized that I had been wrong."

No one wanted to buy the work of an unknown woman artist in the late 1920's, especially one who had not even had a one-man show. The United States had fallen into the grip of the worst depression in history and most Americans were worried about feeding their families and finding enough work to survive the disaster that had befallen the nation.

Day after day Isabel took time away from her painting to carry several small pictures to art dealers who were themselves finding it hard to remain in business. It was a terribly discouraging period for her. The Dudensing Gallery finally took a few of Isabel's paintings on consignment, and a little later on, Alan Gruskin, fresh out of the Fogg Museum at Harvard, founded a gallery in a walk-up railroad flat on Fifth Avenue where Isabel Bishop had her first show. The year was 1932. It was a happy relationship that still exists today—more than four decades later.

In 1934, at the age of 32, Isabel married Harold Wolff, an extraordinary man who became a prominent neurologist. "I felt like an old time professional artist by then," she said. "I was more confident of my work and eager to push ahead." Her husband always respected her determination to pursue art and constantly encouraged Isabel to paint even while they were raising their family. Harold Wolff was just the kind of partner she needed.

13

Even though so much was happening in her professional and private life, Isabel's most trying struggle came from a sincere inner search to break free of Kenneth Hayes Miller's early influence and assimilate instead the many lessons she had learned while studying the great Dutch and Flemish masters, Adrianen Brouwer and Peter Paul Rubens, whose work she had seen in Europe. To develop a uniquely individual style, she drew upon her own experiences, particularly those in Union Square, to create paintings that were—and remain—remarkable for their sensitive and lyrical movement.

Her work has never been considered part of the Social Protest movement, even when she chose Union Square derelicts for subjects. In her opinion, bums are an eccentric lot, not poor men to be pitied. One of the Square's regulars, Walter Broe, proudly modeled for Isabel, Raphael Soyer, and other artists; Broe thought of himself as a professional "hobo." He was especially critical of the poor during the dark days of the Depression. "Why," he said, "they don't even know how to stand in a soup line, they don't have a code either; but as for me—on the merry-go-round of life, I've got the brass ring." "Perhaps," observed Isabel, with her wry sense of humor, "American bums are our only leisure class."

When she paints a man or a woman in a casual setting, she seeks to identify that person's position in society. Each of her fig-ures comes alive and appears to be moving. They are not moving, of course, but the viewer should feel that they *could* move. Isabel Bishop strives to catch the illusive magic of a fleeting instant in time: perhaps two girls sitting at a lunch counter, a woman taking off a coat, or travelers waiting on a subway platform. "I try to paint people who appear to be trivial on the outside and show that they are decent and good inside." In this way she looks upon herself as being somewhat of a "genre" painter, but in a slightly different sense, for she uses people in a more generalized way to create subject matter drawn from her own "intuition and life experience, however special and small."

Today Isabel Bishop loves to sit at the corner window of her Broadway studio high above New York's Union Square and watch the throngs of busy people below. The benches are well-worn and dirty now, the grass has grown thin through years of neglect, and discarded wine bottles, cigarette butts, and old newspapers add a sense of decay to the place.

It is not a pretty sight, it really never has been. Isabel admits that. But she is fascinated by the Square's mysterious beauty. "I feel it is my home," she says. "The Square, with its cheap restaurants and shoddy shops, is a poor business district that hasn't changed in more than forty years; still, as an artist, I am very much at home here."

Her words somehow sound strange, coming as they do from a modest, slightly built, gray haired woman in a neatly starched white smock. Her attractive appearance is more like that of a successful businesswoman than that of an artist. Nevertheless, she is entirely within her element in Union Square and confesses she cannot imagine herself being anywhere else than in this teeming urban milieu "where people just walking around, busy with their lives, make you want to paint."

Perhaps that is because the Square is a microcosm of life itself. Everything appears to be happening there as people come face to face with hope and happiness and suffering and despair. One can see a haggard woman sleeping in misery, with only a torn bag of rags for a pillow; a diligent newspaper reader absorbed in the day's news; children scrambling at play; or a man in a half-drunken stupor watching three friends greedily drink from a brightly colored orange bottle labeled "Screw Driver."

Isabel Bishop's deep personal feelings for these ordinary and often sad human beings has inspired her to create a modern vision of man's human condition. Her best work has a timeless fascination that will never be dated, it will always be fresh and beautiful. But Isabel Bishop has accomplished much more than this: she has overcome the difficulties a woman must surmount to succeed in an occupation long dominated by males, and she did it long before women's rights became a rallying cry.

Martin H. Bush
Wichita State University

Isabel Bishop

Isabel Bishop in her Studio/Photo by Remsen Wolff

I

Isabel Bishop first came to prominence in the thirties, a period once neatly pigeon-holed in a manner suggesting it was dominated and shaped by three men: Thomas Hart Benton, John Stuart Curry and Grant Wood.[1] In the last few years art study has demonstrated that the period was infinitely more complex.[2] It is not our task here to present that period in full, but only to elucidate one major figure from it.

Isabel Bishop, historically, is associated firmly with one of her teachers, Kenneth Hayes Miller, and his most prominent student, Reginald Marsh. The three are sometimes known as the Fourteenth Street School, a reference purely to the location of many of their themes. What they had most in common was an interest in middle class genre painting of New York City scenes. Stylistically, they resemble one another—if generalizations are allowed to shape our judgments. However, examined carefully, Isabel Bishop turns out ultimately to be quite independent of her first influences, and still involved with a growing, developing art. This intimate look is our objective here. In undertaking a close scrutiny, I rely heavily upon four hours of taped discussions with Miss Bishop and, wherever possible, I shall allow her words to tell her story.[3]

Cincinnati born and Detroit raised, young Isabel Bishop arrived in New York in 1918 and entered the New York School of Applied Design for Women, to study illustration:

"When I came to New York . . . I was sixteen or so . . . I came to New York to study commercial art. I was going to be an illustrator, and then I heard of modern art, which I had never heard of in Detroit, Michigan. Why, it opened up something so tremendous that I left the commercial school where I was and went to the (Art Students') League. There things were seething, and I studied a while with Max Weber, and (Guy Pène) du Bois, and so I was very much aware of what was going on."

She studied only a brief time with Weber and, while she admired his work, he made little impact on her artistically. Of du Bois she said: "I think I did get a lot from him, in some way. I didn't study with him very long, but I got to know him and worked in his studio."

Concerning her days at the League and with her chief teacher, Miller, she said: "I was pretty young when I left this commercial school and went to the League. I went to Weber, and Weber was, I thought, a very fine artist but I didn't receive anything from his criticism. Then I went to one of Miller's classes, and I thought, my God, he has a mind! You know at that age though I never went to college, I was reading and I felt myself to be an intellectual. I thought, here was a mind and here I am, I'm home. Though people didn't later realize it, he was entirely sympathetic with the whole modern development. His own work was more or less relating to (Albert P.) Ryder, and he felt that Ryder, Homer and Eakins were *the* three artists of America. I still think that's true. And I think it was about two years or so that I was with him (Miller) and working. Then I left and had a studio of my own on Fourteenth Street (9 West 14th St.). And that's when I did a whole lot of little brown things that I can still look at. I mean, I can still see what I was after.

"Then I really lost my nerve. This idea only came to me recently. I lost my nerve working ... alone. I really felt that I'd have to jump out of the window. So, in order not to do this, I thought I would go back to the League and be there with my peers. ... Miller had ... an advanced composition class which I went into and you know that put me off the track for years! To go back was a wrong move.

"The other day I found some (of those) pictures up here—I slashed them! Why, they are terrible! Now, they were done ... with the utmost earnestness, and I worked on those things and I worked on them, and they were finished, finished things. They were completely off track.

"But sometimes one's colleagues ... are very important. I mean, almost as much so as the teacher. And these colleagues, these other students, and I, I think we took Miller quite wrong. We took him in a wrong sense. He was emphasizing the marvels of the Renaissance and how limited it was to be personal: the recent French emphasis on the uniqueness of each individual is like a sig-nature. Miller felt one should be anonymous, really, in the work, as it were, without individuality. We tried to consider mural problems as something we could collaborate on, and it was totally fallacious; I mean it isn't possible. So I made these labored scenes. They were really just foul. And then I left. ... I had colleagues, and we talked, and we had these ideas about being ... kind of a new Renaissance. It was nonsense, and it was all wrong, and at a point I woke up to this. By Jove, maybe it was du Bois who helped me wake up to it. He came to my studio one time and ... he said, 'My God! What are you doing?'"[4]

Bishop described one of her no longer extant paintings of the early twenties: "It represented an interior with people sitting at card tables and talking with each other, leaning against pillars, and I don't know what all! It was perfectly nonsensical, you know, it made no human sense at all, or any other kind." Mainly what disturbed her later was the cerebral nature of these pictures—Isabel feels strongly that her paintings must relate to life, and these simply did not.

II

Concerning the theoretical ideas she derived from Miller, Bishop told me: "I felt Miller's profundity was very great. It wasn't until I had been studying with him for years that he casually mentioned the name of (Adolph) Hildebrand. Hildebrand wrote a little book called *Problem of Form in Painting and Sculpture* (first published in 1893, standard volume New York, 1945). When I got that book, I discovered that Miller himself had derived his ideas from Hildebrand." She feels that the first successful works she did after reading Hildebrand are the brown-toned canvases and the very early still lifes (figs. 1, 2).

In an attempt to learn more specifically the theories admired and respected by Miss Bishop, I questioned her closely on certain statements made by Hildebrand. For example:

> What the artist has to grapple with is a problem of visual manifestations solely. The subjects which he selects for representation need have neither ethical nor poetic significance. What he does is to give them an esthetic significance which is distinctive and no less valuable.[5]

To this weighty thought Miss Bishop replied: "I think I agree with it, although it was a little limited. I mean it sets out more than it really requires. But after all, this was written at a time when subject matter was all-important. Think of painting in 1893, and think of saying the subject wasn't all-important. This was absolutely revolutionary, and, of course, essentially it is true, but we take it for granted today. We take for granted that in painting, the proportion of form—the element of form, the amount, if you divide it into proportion—to the importance of subject is quite high.

"Now, in poetry, a high proportion of the whole meaning is the form itself. After all, you ask what did the poem say? Well, one would have to recite the poem again. Music—obviously the same is true. Mozart replied when his patron asked 'What does it mean?', 'Oh it means,' and he played it again. In prose the proportion is very high on the side of specific meaning. Now a painting, on the other hand, can have all of the meaning in the form, and can function very strongly."

I pointed out she had just made a defense of abstract art[6]—at one point in our discussion she expressed great admiration for Joseph Albers. However, she said: "I think that abstract art doesn't carry, doesn't deliver quite all the art of painting can deliver. Formal concerns were minimized for so long in painting all during that period—1850's and until 1910. It was assumed that the proportion of the specific meaning of the subject matter in the totality of the content of a painting was high. It isn't, and of course this was what the whole modern movement predicated itself on—the discovery that a very large part of the meaning was in the form, maybe all of it could be."

In response to her answer I again indicated that she had provided a rationale for abstract art, to which she agreed. Yet she asserted subject matter was important to her: "I'm thinking of the whole," she said, "of the range that's possible in art, the range between meaning being totally in the form and being totally in the subject. There is a certain characteristic range in painting, in poetry, in prose, and the range differs in the various arts, I think. As to what point these arts deliver the most they can deliver, I believe this: that abstract art, of course, can have content without subject. But the content is very generalized. It must be. It can be cheerful, it can be melancholy, it can be energetic or restful or exciting, but it couldn't deliver much of your relation to life, your experience although esthetically, it is perfectly sound. Emphasis on illustration robs art of a great power. Power in the art of painting exists at its height with the use of subject—content being within the subject and within the form."

Postulating that striking a balance between abstraction and subject provides a more universal theme, Miss Bishop said: "I can't agree with the way you say it because you speak as though form and content are different, and, of course, they can't be. That is, I think we have to make a distinction between subject and content, because the content is partly of the subject, if there is a subject, and partly in the form. It can't be separated from it any more than in poetic lines. You say 'what does it say?' Well the line itself carries the meaning.

"Hildebrand feels that the image which is flat is of the utmost importance in the perception of space. This must be strong, then the space is read from that image back, and that isn't exactly like a boxlike space." She also noted that she tried to keep her own space "very narrow, very limited, shallow." Hildebrand, according to Miss Bishop, was

paralleling the modern concept of significant form: "I think that his concepts were the same concepts which are the basis of the modern movement. ... A significant form would be form itself."

Hildebrand again: "All periods of artistic endeavor, therefore, must develop a fundamental way of looking from an artistic standpoint at the wealth of varying appearances found in nature."[7] To this Miss Bishop said: "Oh I think that is so true, really, I like this book better than I thought! It seems to me so true ... that a style is a way of taking in the world, it's a way of perceiving it. I think he is talking about style and its fundamental meaning."

I asked her about one particularly provocative statement by Hildebrand:

To perceive in visual terms the third dimension ... we must imagine ourselves as changing our point of view, and as getting merely a succession of disconnected shifting views on the object more or less in profile. Therefore, in imagining a natural scene otherwise than as a visual projection, the expression of kinesthetic ideas by foreshortening, light, shade, color, etc., is unsatisfactory just in so far as its unity is spoiled by its demand for shifting. It is only in the visual projection that these demands cease, and permit the unitary plane picture to produce its full effect unspoiled.[8]

I asked her how this relates to her work. Isabel said: "It relates exactly to my whole painting for fifty years. It relates exactly to it—that is, aiming at an expression which can be read on one plane. Judgments about depth have to be managed by overlapping,

of course, by using the suggestion of diminu-
tion, but little illusion—very little illusion."

III

Isabel Bishop's subject matter has re-
mained fairly constant over the years: working girls (figs. 10–18), people walking on the
street (figs. 7, 53, 55), and nudes (figs. 4–6,
51, 56). Her procedure for working is a slow
and painfully careful one. She begins with
the drawing, first done very small, perhaps,
while walking around in the neighborhood of
her studio. The drawings are reworked,
perhaps carried to wash which would add
the dimension of value. From this point she
moves into etching and, later, aquatint. In
this last form the composition and values are
fully worked out, but the scale of the print is
small compared to the size of the typical
panel she works on. To make the transition,
to possibly suggest things and try different
sizes, she has the drawing or the aquatint
enlarged in a photographic blowup.[9]

As a generalization, we might observe
that her images move from relative clarity in
the thirties and forties, to a more subtle
manner since that time.

Miss Bishop would often get some of the
local girls to pose for her. For example, the
New York *World-Telegram* of February 27,
1936 ran an article about the models for the
Metropolitan Museum's recently acquired
Two Girls. At the time they were asked to
pose by the artist they were waitresses in
Union Square. Bishop said: "It seemed to

me that in order to say what I felt I wanted
to say about them, girls or men had to be
classifiable. I don't think you can classify the
upper middle class. The upper middle class
is not definable in our society, but these
young people are class-marked in the sense
that you understand they are socially limited. But what I feel about them—and I
really do feel strongly about these things—
is that I know so many instances where, if
they want to move, in a social sense, they
can.

"If they want to move into another class
they can, and it's that mobility that con-
nected for me, something which I was absolutely focused on—the attempt to make
forms which to the spectator were mobile or
moveable, that could move. Not that they
were moving. I'm interested in something
else now which is quite different, that is to
say, I am interested in trying to convey
movement taking place.

"There are very few instances in the history of art where mobility and movement
are expressed in the same picture. Now of
course Rubens expressed this and Fragonard I think. Renoir was interested in
mobility and Rembrandt was interested in
mobility. I mean, what he painted had the
potential for movement." I asked for a more
distinct definition of mobility versus movement: "One is the potential," she said, "one
(mobility) is felt as a potential by the onlooker. You feel observing me, that I can
move, though I'm still. You know that I can

23

move. But what tells you that in what you actually see? To express that potential by visual means is a very subtle business. You can't describe it in words, it has to be expressed in the modeling. To express it in the modeling there has to be created in the onlooker—I've found after many, many years experimenting—a sense of physical continuity as by a subtle and delicate web throughout the picture. (This almost invisible web is sensed by the onlooker as a continuity; there ceases to be mobility.)

"But now movement is so different! One of the greatest artists that ever lived, I think, Poussin, creates belief in violent movement without mobility in the individual forms. In such dramatic battle scenes as *The Rape of the Sabines*, movement is truly expressed, it's not just described. It takes place in your nervous system. You experience this battle. But then if you take a position which you're not supposed to as an onlooker, and you say to this soldier (arm raised in a dramatic gesture) 'Move your arm,' you find it breaks off! It can't itself move though it is part of a system where a belief in movement is created. The ballet cannot change. The ballet takes place in the Poussin, but the ballet can't change. Therefore, mobility is not there, though it seems like a contradiction in terms. It's not a matter of verbalism at all, but of experience. Truly movement can take place without mobility, as mobility can be present without movement."

I had difficulty understanding precisely what the distinction between mobility and movement are. I suggested the possibility that Poussin's figures are frozen in time. Bishop said: "They would be frozen if he didn't succeed. But he succeeded in creating, in your nervous system, the belief ... that the movement is taking place."

Returning to her own paintings of figures she continued: "For many years, I was after the mobility and *not* movement. I was after mobility and I felt about these class-marked people that they were mobile in life, and that some of them did move. I've kept track during many years and some have moved in life. Others, of course, haven't, but an emphasis on this possibility seems to me a characteristic of American life."

Clearly, it appeared to me, we were talking about two things: mobility as something in its own right; and mobility implying a certain social consciousness. To this Miss Bishop said: "I was conscious of their being class-marked, but not class-fixed. If I succeeded in making them seem to the onlooker that they could turn and move in a physical sense, this opened up a subjective potential which could include the mobility of content. I mean it made it possible to suggest, or at least the suggestion was already there, to my mind, that if a physical movement takes place who can tell what other kind of movement might take place."

As to why she stayed with this particular kind of working woman: "Perhaps because they were available." What about the lower classes: "I've been interested in bums and so on for years (fig. 9). I was interested because I could get them. One of them would just knock on my door and say: 'Well, if you need me I'll be under the horse's tail' (referring to an equestrian monument of General Washington in Union Square). And I'd get him ... and bring him in. They were available, and they were very beautiful in the sense that their clothes were so beautiful to draw. But in their social class ... I didn't feel they were victims exactly, but that their lives were largely a matter of choice." Pressing the point on the meaning of class-marked: Bishop admires Renoir greatly, she pointed out that when Renoir painted a bourgeois young woman holding a cup of chocolate, one knows "exactly what her mother was like, what her grandmother was like, and what her great-grandmother was like, and one knows what her children would be like." In France, unlike America, there was social continuity. This American lack of continuity "is one reason portrait paintings are impossible or shallow in this country: there is no categorizing of a person beyond his own physiognomy." Is she politically inclined in this type of picture? "Not at all. I had no political interest whatever. These were observations of fact, as I felt, it of American life. I felt I was saying some small thing which was true of American life—apart from politics or economics."

A theme that preoccupies Isabel Bishop from the early 1930's (figs. 7, 53, 55) to the present time is that of a group passing on the street. Earlier renditions showed people drawn from the same social class as the genre pictures of young women. But now they are young college students. Gone, from the 1960's onward, are the shop girls talking, eating, or hanging on subway straps: "The people I'm using are younger people. To my mind they're in the situation of the students, with a reason to be moving in a certain place and time. But my feeling is that they are in a temporary role which relates them in some subjective way." The fact they are students helps unify the subject thematically, but these people have no connection, emotionally or psychologically, with one another: "No," Miss Bishop said, "they don't, and that is part, I'll agree, of what I'm interested in.

"But that they don't know each other, of course, is necessary to what I want. I don't know why, but what I am fascinated with is the miracle that this movement takes place at all. This came to me most forcefully after I'd been in Maine for two weeks. I never go away in the summer, but I went to Maine ... a charming place, and when I came back here I thought, my God, the incredible richness of this ... coming and going of people, and the miraculous thing that they could change places showing that the air must be as palpable, that the air is as positive as they are. There must be a total unity in which this can take place, and to make it take place for the onlooker is my wish. I search for, and do not find as yet, a way or ways to make the onlooker feel that something is taking place right there, with a change of position of people. Not in relation in their coming together or going apart, but just their moving. Well, it seems miraculous to me. Why is that? It seems to me like a ballet. I mean, I look out that window and these people move, like a ballet!"

I remarked that all these people seem as if they were caught in a moment of time. "That's what I hope you won't feel. ..." She was specific in desiring some sense of movement: "I would feel it a total failure unless there was some element of movement. ..." How does one arrive at that sensation? Bishop responded simply: "Well, I just keep trying." She proceeded, "That's the reason I try all these ways and I don't know how, but this problem keeps me going on. I don't know of anybody who wanted to do this. You see, anybody could have done it much better than I if they had wanted to. I don't know of anybody who wants it, so I feel like an explorer, you see, and I want something, and maybe nobody, anybody, else would want to do it. ... So I keep trying it, to find some way, and it keeps me tearing down here to my studio every morning."

Miss Bishop has tried, occasionally, to place seated figures among the walking ones (fig. 151). And to her this inclusion makes the problem for her "very different." About this variant she said, "To have still people and moving people is awfully hard anyway. I mean, it's hard for me subjectively to make it real, to make it viable. But then sitting, is another element of disparateness. If everything is moving, that's one situation. Most people moving, one standing, that's another. But if some are sitting, that seems to me everyway, philosophically and subjectively, different.

"Now I don't mean philosophically in the technical sense. I only mean in my feeling that movement, if it takes place at all, has to be conceived of as a totality. I don't think that movement can take place against a still background; one must feel the world is moving. When I stand at my window at Union Square, it gives me great inspiration because movement is from so many directions. I find what I have to do is to keep my head turning so that I don't just see the people moving against something, but the whole situation turning."

I wonder why these people are so unaware of each other. I look at a particular figure and she stares ahead with an intentness, almost a determination, not to be aware. To this Bishop said: "Yes, I think that is part of my subject, really, that she is definitely unaware, that her movement is not in relation to awareness of others. In the painting the modeling relates them. Psychologically they are not either pulling apart or together. It is part of the fascination of this subject to try to create the sensation of these two people coming toward each other and these two moving apart, as one part of feeling the modeling of it. ..."

Are there layers of meaning in such pictures, I ask? "No," Bishop said, "simply it is the coming and going that fascinates me, but

I feel that it is necessary within myself, to think of them as having a role which they share."

Almost from the beginning Isabel Bishop painted nudes along with her other subject interests. In the nude her admiration for Fragonard, Rubens, Renoir and Rembrandt is clearly manifested. Her nudes are never pretty in the ordinary sense. Quite to the contrary, they are of the corpulent type preferred by Rubens and Renoir. Incidentally, her nudes are only of women, and she does them because "the female nude is a tradition." She went on: "I have no sexual interest in females. But the tradition is of the female nude, it is not only a subject but an art form as Kenneth Clark said.[10] In other words, one would have to have a rather special attitude to study the male nude."

IV

Artist Isabel Bishop has been a tireless worker for the approximately fifty years she has produced independently. At her Riverdale home in the Bronx, she lives as the widow of Dr. Harold George Wolff—each day she travels to her studio on Union Square in lower Manhattan, where she puts on her smock and is Bishop the artist. Part of this tremendous commitment to her work, as well as her feeling that the work must be done in New York, surely comes from Kenneth H. Miller. Of her former mentor she wrote:

Kenneth Hayes Miller's presence on Fourteenth Street, New York City, was a fact of solid importance to many artists who seldom climbed the stairs to his studio. For one thing, he was always there. While others from this place tried living in New Mexico, Paris, Seattle, Italy, Maine, or, at any rate, were actually in New York but a few months of the year, Miller just stayed. And he became a symbol. The physical presence of one painter, among the thousands in New York City, however, even the fact he *was* always to be found, and in the same spot, year after year, in season and out of season, wouldn't mean very much in itself. But two other kinds of steadfastness were present there. One, he was always working. That is, a visit at any time of the day or of the year would unfailingly find him engrossed in the making of a picture. Whether this consistent unvarying application was ideal as a creative method, who can say? But this kind of steadfastness added to the symbol.

The potency of the symbol came mostly, however, from a deeper steadfastness—from an unchanging and fanatically held belief that radiated from him, perceived, I think, by susceptible students as an aura. This belief was that the pursuit of the Art of Painting is of an *absolute* importance, dependent not at all for its validity as a life commitment, on the degree of talent in the pursuer, or any circumstance whatever.[11]

The earliest work in this exhibition (figs. 1, 2) relates to the "brown things" I saw at her studio. They may be characterized as standing out with a clarity and solidity also evident in most of her pictures of the thirties. The intention here is to describe actuality— but with the classical sculptural simplicity expressed by Miller about the same time:

The power of Miller's work lies ... in an observation of life that reaches down to its deeper, more pervasive, and continuous structure of broad, weighty forms carefully integrated with surface detail.[12]

Except for some exquisitely sensitive still lifes (figs. 2, 3), thematically, Bishop's work expresses the dual image of shop girls at leisure. Executed in dark tonalities, the images clear, but not as linear as the *Self Portrait*, these young women are always shown at ease, never in working situations. The explanation for this is simple since Isabel roamed Union Square catching glimpses of them during off times. For example, concerning a series of works showing people drinking from a public water fountain (fig. 48), she wrote:

> I've got pages and pages of sketches of men and girls drinking out of that fountain ... You know most people lift one leg when they drink. Some put their hands behind them. Others embrace the bowl. But it's so quick and nice—like birds, they drink and fly away— and I have a devil of a time. You could easily pose a person there, of course, but that wouldn't be it. I struggle for months and months to make it look as momentary as it really is.[13]

Also from this period are a few powerfully conceived individual heads such as *The Kid*. In the strong modeling of the partial figure, Bishop comes closest to her colleague Reginald Marsh—the head crowds the format. Related to this painting is a somewhat more delicate drawing (fig. 69). Here, there is a sense of atmosphere surrounding the head, small in comparison to the space it occupies. In the works there becomes an interesting duet in forcefulness and delicacy.

The earliest painting I've been able to discover of a female nude is *Seated Nude*, 1934 (fig. 7). Done in warm earth tones, there is an almost Rembrandtesque air about it. Then, too, we must be conscious of how alert Miss Bishop is to 17th-century art. Even as the study of a nude it falls into the area of genre painting: this is no idealized type, but rather a corpulent young woman observed as she examines one of her feet. Perhaps it would not be too much of an exaggeration to infer that here is one of the shop girls stripped of her clothing. I do not mean that we are made to feel the lady is naked—she is nude in the way Kenneth Clark describes nudity as distinct from nakedness.[14]

As usual, the drawings associated with this painting have a more immediate impact on the viewer: they are done with such flawless skill capturing the essence of a pose. Also interesting is the fact that they differ in pose from the completed painting. Miss Bishop explored a wide number of possibilities before deciding on this painting. Any wonder her painting output rarely exceeds three or four a year.

There remains one other major figure painting for this decade—*Waiting*, 1938 (fig. 68). Here the contrast of the mother's large proportions to the small form of the child sleeping with its head on her lap tells the story of *Waiting* completely: bored wakefulness and exhaustion. The composition is contained within a triangular arrangement bestowing on it something of the monumentality Miller was looking for in his work—

with this difference: Bishop's linearity, the clear edges, are beginning to soften as the decade progresses, and parts melt into the atmosphere of the whole.

Critical response to Bishop comes in spurts since she has had few exhibitions, and those widely separated in time. However, in 1935 the Midtown gave her a show and critics had the opportunity of reacting to her latest works. The range of critical response ran the entire gamut from branding her a follower of Miller to seeing some special qualities in Bishop that emerge and give notice of her originality. One art reviewer who found in her an extension of her teacher wrote:

Like Kenneth Hayes Miller, with whom she studied, Miss Bishop seeks her material in the lower part of Manhattan, picking out shop girls, subway riders and the mixed collection of humanity gathering on New York's squalid avenue of shoppers, Fourteenth Street. Her color is also akin to the pallid tones of Miller's art, as are her portly faced female subjects.[15]

One article accused her of too much solidity in her figures, but one of the most perceptive observations was made by Henry McBride:

She is not interested in flights of the imagination or disturbing problems ... but is content, apparently, to refine upon her observation and add to the subtlety of her expression. This eminently painter-like, if modest, aim has produced its reward, for she has never appeared to greater advantage than in her present display. With increasing assurances her style has loosened up somewhat; *she is no longer afraid to lose a contour on occasion, with the result a gain in atmospheric en-velope, and fluidity. And all this without any loss of solidity.*[16] (Italics added)

Art News expressed the belief that in Bishop's work there is "a heart-felt desire to grasp the beauty of dismal middle-class and down-and-out settings and subjects, and all this to the good."[17] But it was Emily Genauer who announced the arrival of a major artist on the scene:

Isabel Bishop, we say with vehemence and conviction, is one of the *most important woman painters* in America today. There are perhaps a half dozen others in her class, though we cannot honestly think at the moment of that many who are comparable.[18] (Italics added)

The critical attention given her 1935 exhibition clearly illustrated her stature in the New York art world. She showed, along with Milton Avery, Tamayo, and others, at the 1939 New York World's Fair in the American Art Today Building. She exhibited under the auspices of a newly formed group called the Society of Modern Artists. A year before, the Pennsylvania Academy bought her *Young Woman* out of their own show of American art, and the same picture had been shown at the Carnegie International in 1937.

Four years after the 1935 exhibition, at Midtown Galleries, another was mounted. The critics, still mostly responsive to her work, began to note the increasing atmospheric quality in Bishop's art: "She is now," Forbes Watson observed, "...a highly individual exponent of the art of painting." He went on:

...yet it does seem as if such extremely close searching for subtle values sometimes leads this artist to over-see the focal point of her picture. Perhaps it also leads to a vagueness of color, a neutrality approaching timidity. She has such remarkable abilities that one wonders if they would gain or lose by a slightly cleaner and more outward color statement.[19]

Edward Alden Jewell was less kind: "An uncommon amount of squinting failed to bring the Bishop panels into focus and convincing reality."[20] McBride wrote: "Someday the artist may wriggle free from the ocean of Indian red and burnt sienna and do a picture entirely in the primary colors. When this happens the Art Students' League will probably give her a banquet."[21] But she was being collected: the Springfield Museum purchased *The Noon Hour* out of their own biennial; and in 1940, the Butler Art Institute purchased *Laughing Head*. The 1939 Bishop exhibition catalogue reveals paintings were priced from $350 to $900.

The 1940's and 1950's are basically characterized, in terms of subject matter, as adding nothing new (except toward the end of the '50's). Stylistically, they became looser, infinitely more painterly—a direction still regretted by Mr. Jewell. Of her graphics he said: "In most of this work the subjects are clearly, sometimes very tellingly and poignantly portrayed—*a virtue that ... Miss Bishop's paintings do not always possess.*"[22] (Italics added) Despite Mr. Jewell's reservations about her painting, Isabel Bishop was elected a full academician at the National Academy of Design on April 24, 1941, at the age of thirty-nine.

Recognition does not necessarily provide financial independence, Bishop told a reporter for the Worcester, Mass. *Telegram.* She wrote:

If you're planning to become an artist so you can pile up a fortune you better get some advice from Isabel Bishop, one of the leading painters in the country.... Miss Bishop ... admits that if it were not for the small sum of money left her in a will and the income of her husband, Dr. Harold G. Wolff ... she would have real trouble following her art career.[23]

She confided in me recently that in all the years she has been working, only the last three would provide her enough to live on. Her financial situation, if there had been no family money, might not have prevented her from pursuing a career. She would, however, have had to do as countless others; teach.

Bishop has produced numerous drawings over the years almost universally well-received and praised, even by those who held reservations about her paintings. In 1942 the Midtown Galleries had a Bishop drawing show. Henry McBride responded avidly:

This artist has a nervous, sensitive line, an instinctive grasp of form, the ability to make figures exist even when in shadow and quite a few other graces of a technical order, none which are allowed to interfere with the essential vitality of the people she depicts. Her fellow artists may admire her restraint, her refusal to make loud statements, and her conservative but very sure way of arranging a composition, but the outsiders who are only vaguely aware of these matters will, nevertheless, recognize and appreciate the closeness to life of Miss Bishop's observations. The young men and women in the drawings belong to the great middle class, the class that takes the 8 a.m. subway to work, that gulps hot dogs at street corners, goes to lesser movies, and does a little discreet lovemaking on the benches in the park. They may have some occasional troubles but Miss Bishop doesn't specialize in those. Her people are glad to be alive and ... particularly glad to be New Yorkers.[24]

Another reviewer credited the artist with revealing "a penetrative insight into the lives of these working girls."[25] Finally, the drawing show elicited this response from the *Brooklyn Eagle*:

> This reviewer's theory is that it is such talents as Miss Bishop's which bring the exponents of the conservative past up to date, in tune with the communicable now. While Miss Bishop's drawings are essentially painter's drawings, filled with color suggestion without the use of color, they reveal the basis of her distinguished paintings. They are convincingly arranged and reveal the essence of life and character.[26]

I told Isabel Bishop that on the basis of the proportion of drawings and prints to paintings, I could make a case for considering her essentially a graphic artist. This conclusion she objected to strongly; she envisions herself as a painter who also draws and etches. Accepting this view of herself we might select here a few of the outstanding pictures of the '40's and '50's, which do seem to shape a coherent stylistic grouping.

It might also be appropriate at this point to describe the artist's technical approach to painting:

> Painting ... is built up in a Renaissance technique of underpainting, then layer on layer of careful pigment, color blended with color, resulting in a smooth finish and ripeness of effect.
> Miss Bishop works on composition gesso panels ... with an underpainting in grey. When she finishes the painting process, and in her case it is a slow one, she frequently accents her forms with pencil lines easily visible against the oil, and this habit manages to be effective along with her pale tonality.[27]

It is probably true to say that Miss Bishop has very little theoretical views on color. She told me she expects color to add to the liveliness of the picture and judges the color in regard to its effectiveness in this intent. In addition, she showed me a volume on *Chinese Art* (New York, 1927) containing one hundred color plates. Miller told her about this book. If her paintings looked "right" against the color of these plates, she judged them a success: "You can test it (color)," she said, "if you put up this (color plate) and you put a painting next to it. If it chimes with the painting, if you can imagine they're existing in the same room, then I know that it's acceptable—what I'm doing in color."[28]

The paintings of the '40's are notable for lack of any recognition of the War. In fact, for the most part, the pictures of that decade and the next still deal with familiar scenes—the girls are the same, only their clothing style has changed. From an earlier time are two figure renditions of shop girls at their pastimes—eating ice cream cones (figs. 15, 19, 22), or stuffing food into their

31

mouths (fig. 31). Paintings like *Resting* (fig. 26) and *The Long Wait* are successors to *Waiting*.

However, a new touch is added going underground to the subway. Here, the girls are now bored and yawning, leaning against a pillar reading a paper (figs. 24, 30), or in a train holding to the straps (fig. 34). They look exhausted, as they await the long trip home. These, however, still fall into the realm of genre, with the location shifted.

But in two remarkable paintings of the late '50's (fig. 35), she transcends that label. Both show the subway interior at Union Square. The people depicted in these are relatively minor factors, either physically or psychologically, standing on the various layers of the train platform. What *Subway Scene* and the lesser known *Union Square* share is an emphasis on formal, right angle structure forced on them by the nature of the subject. The Whitney Museum's version adds the dimension of a reflected image in the mirror of a candy machine that is occupying the center foreground of the composition. This reflected person is on our side of the picture surface—strange considering the artist's exaggerated respect for the surface of the painting. Be that as it may, from this time to the present, the tremendous energy she has to give her work has gone into pictures in which narrative is relegated to an insignificant degree. She told me she no longer thinks of herself as a genre painter.

From this time, also, are three nudes (figs. 7, 25, 27), the finest of which appears to me to be the small painting in the Roby Collection. She is a direct descendant of the Whitney's painting, executed with a surprising solidity. Incidentally, Miss Bishop mentioned that she prefers canvas to panel for the nudes—something about the texture of the canvas that envokes the sense of flesh. Ten years later—*Undressing* (fig. 36)—even the nude is caught in the web of her vaporous painting style.

In 1949, after ten years, the Midtown Galleries had another Bishop exhibition. Again she attracted wide critical response:

> Isabel Bishop is a good draughtsman and a skillful, careful and evidently slow worker; the first exhibition of her paintings in ten years is a tribute to the pre-emptive value which public and private collectors put on her work. She paints with a realism which is sensitive to the psychology and atmosphere of her subjects, and in a style to which non-objective technique offers but few attractions, but which all the same can sometimes be accused of monotony.[29]

She was frequently held up as representing a viable alternative to the then emerging Abstract Expressionist art:

> Appearing at a time of slipshod technical standards, her craftsmanship deserves careful study. ... These means are complex and the end fully justifies them, *for they give the commonplace subjects a poetic gravity that they could scarcely find in themselves.*[30] (Italics added)

Interestingly, Miss Bishop admires the Abstract Expressionists, and regrets they never invited her to The Club to argue ideas.[31]

Finally, Margaret Breuning wrote a perceptive review of the 1949 exhibition:

> While many contemporary artists appear definitely under 'influences,' this painter has developed an aesthetic idiom which is entirely personal, in an unusual combination of precise draftsmanship and loose brushwork. It has been asserted that her canvases lack color and attain a monotony of impression. Yet if anyone looks at this showing, he must be impressed with the color in these paintings, so delicately modulated that one hue melts into another in harmonious relation to the structure of the design. The figures of her canvases are drawn from the environing life, neither romanticized nor understated, but imaginatively presented in the natural milieu.[32]

Henry McBride's respect for Bishop's work grew with the years. He called her "a careful and scholarly draftsman and a careful and scholarly observer of life."[33] The artist herself was quoted as having stated: "I try to limit content, to limit everything . . . in order to get down to something."

Between shows, Bishop would occasionally attract attention through an article such as "Bishop Paints a Picture," in *Art News* in 1951. Here Dorothy Seckler very observantly recorded Bishop's love affair with the picture surface:

> The habit of keeping the surface of the pictures pristine—only lightly developing it during the exploratory period—is a striking characteristic of Miss Bishop's method. For some time the panel will play the role of a kind of alter ego to the probing and disheveled sketches and studies, and it constantly serves as a reminder of the jealous presence of two-dimensional space.[34]

An incident worth recording occurred about 1953—the formation of a group calling themselves Reality, which was also the name of the publication they sponsored. Through the initiative of Raphael Soyer, Isabel Bishop met with a group of artists which included Kuniyoshi, Levine and Ben Shahn. Bishop said, "They were in great revolt against the usurping of the whole art scene by the Abstract Expressionists." She continued:

> They were really up in arms, and I always felt that the word 'Reality' was wrong, and that wasn't the right name, because, what do you mean 'Reality?' Jack Levine suggested, but they wouldn't do it, to call it 'From the Horse's Mouth.'
> We used to meet, and I loved those meetings because I loved those people! And they were very earnest, and Ben Shahn was very wrought up because he had been through the out-country and he found that colleges were teaching, that the students didn't know there had been any art before Abstract Expressionism. They didn't know about tradition.
> So we were very exercised about this and we made this little paper expressing our views and four issues were all we made, and we stopped meeting.[35]

A reviewer in the *Los Angeles Times*, after publication of the first issue of *Reality*, No. 1, 1953, sought the essence of its meaning:

It objected to 'the arbitrary exploitation of a single phase of painting' (viz.: 'mere textural novelty') and the jargon in which it is discussed. It questioned that 'the excitation of texture and color' are the true ends of art. 'The commonest and most wrong advice to a young painter,' wrote one of its artist contributors, 'is to look inward to express himself. Most of all he needs to look outward to understand.'[36]

Bishop had an article in the first issue linking the avant-garde of that day with the academy, an argument often heard during this period. However, she felt that they shared a sense of the self-righteous "and have a great sense of mission. In their rigidity and intolerance, in the certainty of each that he has all the answers, they show their spiritual brotherhood."

Isabel Bishop may have been giving a more balanced view of her attitudes in these notes for a lecture given later in the decade:

For the revolt that was 'modern' took place only yesterday. And it did in the beginning aim at the living tradition and thus produced many immortal works. Even in its congealed state, present art forms are much superior to those beloved by Academies which are still further removed from the Tradition. Perhaps it is the essence of the living tradition that must always be discovered, that any clue is painfully won and then only relevant at a moment of time, and never to be passed on. This problem of education is a severe one. But dogmatism is no solution. The health of education depends on freedom to question all assumptions, certainly those not well hidden in the supposed 'standards' of the reactionaries and also those behind the set of dogma now called 'Art of our Century.'[37]

She repeated this argument in the second issue of *Reality*.

Turning to Isabel Bishop's work since 1960, Lawrence Campbell saw what was to come in 1955: "Her subject is one most present-day artists avoid: the modern fragmented city and the people who live in it, yet are not altogether of it."[38] There are still some nudes (figs. 38, 42), done in the exquisite late manner, but the Fourteenth Avenue shop girls are not to be found. Instead, the dominant subject, as she herself has so passionately pointed out, is the young college student.

The significance of this new subject is that it elicited fresh artistic means. If her style was vaporous before, it remains so, but now fitted into a perceivable structure. This is a structure of abstract planes in which the walker is set against and enmeshed at the same time. Despite her unwillingness to admit to any symbolic interpretations of these paintings, certainly these psychologically isolated people caught in their orangey worlds, imply something of the impersonality and loneliness of life in America.

As early as 1960, one critic began to note the change:

The figures have lost their solid earthiness, have been melted by light and loose brushwork into pointillist presences slipping in and out of a background that now is strengthened and emphasized.[39]

John Canaday wrote Bishop in a letter dated April 29, 1967:

I have thought that perhaps your technical

device that I describe inadequately as 'dots and lines' was intended to give to the subjects a kinetic character, some of the feeling of constant motion and change to which people in the city are subjected even when they are nominally at rest.

Art News reacted in a similar fashion:

She traps her subjects in a network of shimmering lines, dots and strokes. Often you can see right through her figures and yet they remain substantial. She is trying for mobility in the Baroque sense: the form fluid and moving. Therefore, stance and gesture are important and, in observing pedestrians, she has formed a kind of city dance.[40]

"It's magical," Isabel said, "to look out my studio window ... the people going past each other ... the movement ... like an unconscious ballet."[41]

One of the great cultural historians of our times is Louis Mumford. In a letter to Bishop he summed up her qualities and meaning as an artist and I will let his words close this study:

A few days ago I wandered into the show of American Woman Painters at Mt. Holyoke, which contained the usual vast canvases screaming with emptiness. At the end of my tour, I came upon three pictures that halted me; and imagine my surprise when I found that two of them were by you. By ill-luck I've seen none of your recent work for years and years; so it was the art—though on reflection I could perceive the kinship between your earlier and your present style, which has gained strength in its muted perfection of statement, and has lost nothing.[42]

Sheldon Reich
Professor of Art History
University of Arizona

NOTES

1. I'd like to acknowledge my debt to Mr. William E. Steadman for providing me the opportunity of writing this essay. In addition, my profound gratitude for unstinting cooperation goes to Isabel Bishop and Mary Gruskin.

2. William C. Agee, "The 1930's: An Unknown Chapter in American Art," unidentified clipping in the possession of the Midtown Galleries.

3. The interviews were held March 18 and 19, 1974. All Bishop quotations, unless otherwise indicated, are from these interviews. Miss Bishop did edit her statements for the purpose of publication.

4. Being more specific about the ideas imparted by Miller, Bishop said: "He said a picture should read toward the spectator, and ... that is an absolute fallacy. It took me years to find that out."

5. Hildebrand, Adolph, p. 14.

6. In all fairness, Miss Bishop often stated her acceptance of abstract art. Her enmity was directed against those who would not consider any other kind of art legitimate.

7. Hildebrand, p. 19.

8. *Ibid.* p. 31.

9. See Dorothy Seckler, "Bishop Paints a Picture," *Art News*, L (Nov. 1951), pp. 38-41, 63-64.

10. Kenneth Clark, *The Nude* (New York, 1959).

11. Typed essay, probably from 1952, intended for *Art Digest.*

12. Lincoln Rothschild, *To Keep Art Alive* (Philadelphia, 1974), p. 42.

13. "They Drink and Fly Away," *Time* (May 29, 1949), p. 69.

14. Clark, *The Nude*, Chapter I: "The Naked and the Nude."

15. *Art Digest* (Feb. 15, 1936), p. 19.

16. *New York Sun*, Feb. 15, 1936.

17. Ann H. Sayre, "Substantial Technique in Isabel Bishop's Work," *Art News* (Feb. 22, 1936), p. 18.

18. *New York World Telegram*, Feb. 15, 1936.

19. Forbes Watson, "Isabel Bishop," *Magazine of Art* (Jan. 1939), pp. 53-54.

20. Edward Alden Jewell, *Art Digest* (Feb. 1, 1939), p. 21.

21. *Ibid.*

22. *New York Times*, May 19, 1942.

23. Donna Ford, May 20, 1941.

24. *New York Sun*, May 22, 1942.

25. "The Bishop Girl Seen in Drawing Show," *Art Digest* (June 1942), p. 14.

26. *Brooklyn Eagle*, May (?) 24, 1942.

27. Sayre, *Art News* (Feb. 22, 1936), p. 18.

28. Bishop interviews.

29. Christopher E. Freemantle, "New York Commentary," *Studio* (Sept. 1949), p. 91.

30. *New York Times*, July 8, 1949.

31. See Dore Ashton, *The New York School* (New York, 1972), pp. 98f.

32. *Art Digest* (May 1, 1949), p. 15.

33. *New York Sun*, May 26, 1949.

34. Seckler, *Art News* (Nov. 1951), pp. 38-41, 63-64.

35. Bishop interviews.

36. Arthur Miller, "Real Questions Lost in 'Reality' Debate," *Los Angeles Times*, July 26, 1953.

37. From the Isabel Bishop archive at the Archives of American Art.

38. Lawrence Campbell, *Art News* (Nov. 1955), p. 50.

39. *New York Herald-Tribune*, May 7, 1960.

40. Ralph Pomeroy, "Isabel Bishop," *Art News* (April 1966), p. 9.

41. Lee Sheridan, Springfield, Mass. *Daily News*, Feb. 20, 1974.

42. Louis Mumford, Letter dated April 29, 1962.

Illustrations

1. SELF-PORTRAIT—1927
   Oil
   14 x 13

2. BOTTLES—1931
Oil
17 x 20

3. STILL LIFE WITH BOTTLES—n.d.
   Oil
   18½ x 36½

4. UNION SQUARE—c. 1932
Oil
14 x 17⅜

5. DANTE AND VIRGIL IN UNION SQUARE—1932
   Oil
   27 x 52

6. ON THE STREET (14th Street)—1932
   Oil
   14½ x 26

7. NUDE—1934
   Oil on Composition Board
   33 x 40

8. THE CLUB—1935
Oil and Tempera
20 x 24

9. STOOPING MAN—1936
Oil
12 x 10

10. LAUGHING HEAD—1938
Oil
13 x 12

11. TIDYING UP—c. 1938
    Oil on Masonite
    15 x 11½

12. WAITING—1938
Oil and Tempera on Gesso Panel
29 x 22½

13. TWO GIRLS WITH A BOOK—1938
    Oil and Tempera on Gesso Panel
    20 x 24

14. OFFICE GIRLS—1939
Oil on Masonite
36 x 22

15. LUNCH HOUR—1939
Oil on Panel
27 x 17½

16. AT THE NOON HOUR—1939
Tempera and Pencil on Composition Board
25 x 18

17. ENCOUNTER—1940
    Oil and Tempera
    23¾ x 15¾

18. TAKING OFF HER COAT—c. 1941
Oil on Board
13⅞ x 8

19. ICE CREAM CONES—1942
   Oil and Tempera on Masonite
   34 x 20

20. STRAP HANGERS—c. 1943
Oil and Tempera on Gesso Panel
20 x 16

21. RESTING—1943
Oil on Gesso Panel
16 x 17

22. TWO GIRLS OUTDOORS—1944
Oil
30 x 18

23. MENDING—1945
   Oil on Composition Board
   25 x 16½

24. GIRL READING NEWSPAPER—1946
Oil
29 x 18

25. NUDE IN INTERIOR—1947
Oil and Tempera
21 x 18

26. DOUBLE DATE DELAYED—1948
Oil on Board
22⅛ x 18⅛

27. NUDE BENDING—1949
Oil and Tempera
21 x 24

28. HOMEWARD—1951
   Oil and Tempera
   26 x 20

29. INTERLUDE—1953
Oil and Tempera on Gesso Panel
34 x 20

30. GIRLS IN THE SUBWAY STATION—1953
    Oil and Tempera on Gesso Panel
    32 x 20

31. SNACK BAR—c. 1954
   Oil on Panel
   13½ x 11⅛

32. PAUSE TO REFRESH—1955
Oil and Tempera on Gesso Panel
30½ x 16⅛

33. THE BATHER—c. 1955
Tempera
18 x 21

34. SUBWAY READING—1956
Oil
24½ x 17¾

35. SUBWAY SCENE—1957–58
Tempera and Oil on Gesso Panel
40 x 28

36. UNDRESSING—1959
   Oil
   33 x 29½

37. STUDY FOR "SODA FOUNTAIN WITH PASSERS BY"—1960
Oil and Tempera
13¼ x 23

38. UNDRESSING ON THE BED—1960
   Oil and Tempera on Gesso Panel
   18½ x 37

39. STUDY FOR "UNDRESSING ON THE BED"—1960
   Oil
   19 x 38

40. COKE BREAK—1960
Oil and Tempera on Board
29⅜ x 20½

41. SODA FOUNTAIN WITH PASSERS BY—1960
   Oil and Tempera
   24 x 36

42. WOMAN UNDRESSING—1961
Oil and Tempera on Masonite
20¼ x 34

43. WOMEN WALKING #2—1963
Oil and Tempera
27½ x 30½

44. WALKING IN THE SUBWAY STATION—1963
Oil and Tempera
24 x 33

45. PREPARATION—1964
   Oil and Tempera
   22 x 20

46. LITTLE NUDE—1964
   Oil
   26½ x 21¼

47. NUDE REACHING—1964
Oil and Tempera
28 x 35

48. STUDY FOR "DRINKING FOUNTAIN"—1965
Oil
15 x 12

49. GETTING DRESSED—1966
Oil and Tempera
22 x 20

50. STUDENTS WALKING—1967
Oil and Tempera
31½ x 48

51. FIVE WOMEN WALKING #1—1967
Oil and Tempera on Gesso Panel
31½ x 39½

52. SKETCH—STUDY FOR "THE COATS"—1967
Oil and Tempera on Gesso Panel
28 x 30

53. FIVE WOMEN WALKING #2—c. 1967
Oil on Board
32 x 40

54. SEATED NUDE—1967
Oil and Tempera on Gesso Panel
23 x 21

55. STUDENTS WALKING #2—1968
   Oil and Tempera
   31½ x 48

56. SUBWAY STATION UNDER GRAND CENTRAL #2—1968
   Oil on Gesso Panel
   27 x 46

57. STREET SCENE—1969
   Oil and Tempera
   16½ x 23

58. MEN AND GIRLS WALKING—c. 1970
Oil on Masonite
28½ x 39½

59. STUDENTS—1971
Oil
29 x 40

60. CAMPUS STUDENTS #2—1972
   Oil and Tempera
   34 x 38½

61. HIGH SCHOOL STUDENTS—1973
  Oil
  25 x 40

62. WOMAN SEATED FACING LEFT (Study for Soda Fountain)—n.d.
Pen and Ink
11⅞ x 8½

63. WOMAN SEATED FACING RIGHT (Study for Soda Fountain)—n.d.
Pen and Ink
11⅜ x 7⅜

64. STUDY FOR "THE BOOTBLACK"—c. 1931–32
Watercolor
19⅜ x 16½

65. VIRGIL AND DANTE IN UNION SQUARE—1932
Pencil Drawing
13 x 26

66. "TWO GIRLS," STUDY—1934
Ink
9¼ x 6

67. STUDY FOR "THE CLUB"—1935
Wash, Chalk, Pencil and Oil
16½ x 19¾

68. WAITING—1935
Pen, Ink and Wash
7⅛ x 6

69. ROSALYND—1936
Ink and Wash
4 x 3

70. THE DAY'S NEWS—c. 1936
Ink
5¼ x 4

71. NUDE SEATED—1938
   Ink Wash
   5⅞ x 6⅝

72. ICE CREAM CONES—c. 1938–39
Pen and Ink Wash
8 x 5

73. TWO GIRLS—c. 1941
Gouache Drawing
17 x 23

74. CARD GAME—1942
Watercolor
17⅞ x 18⅞

75. ICE CREAM CONES—1940
Pencil with White Crayon
35¾ x 21½

76. SEATED NUDE—c. 1945
    Ink and Wash
    7 x 6½

77. GIRL TAKING OFF SWEATER—1970
Ink Wash
6½ x 4½

78. STUDY FOR "COKE BREAK"—A—c. 1960
Pen and Ink
7½ x 4⅛

79. STUDY FOR "COKE BREAK"—B—c. 1960
Pen and Ink
7½ x 4⅛

80. STUDY FOR "COKE BREAK"—C—c. 1960
Pen and Ink
7½ x 4½

81. STUDY FOR "COKE BREAK"—D—c. 1960
Pen and Ink
6¾ x 4½

82. STUDY FOR "COKE BREAK"—E—c. 1960
Pen and Ink
7 x 4½

83. STUDY FOR "COKE BREAK"—F—c. 1960
Pen and Ink
6¾ x 4½

84. STUDY FOR "COKE BREAK"—G—c. 1960
Pen and Ink
6¼ x 3¾

85. STUDY FOR "COKE BREAK"—H—c. 1960
Pen and Ink
5½ x 4¼

86. STUDY FOR "COKE BREAK"—I—c. 1960
Pen and Ink
6¼ x 3¼

87. NUDE—1925
   Etching
   6½ x 5⅝

88. NUDE—1925
   Etching
   10 x 6¾
   Inscribed: To Walter Fillin with Warm Greetings

89. IN FRONT OF 42nd STREET LIBRARY—1925
Etching
3 x 4

90. OVER THE WALL—1927
Etching
2½ x 3½

91. LEANING ON THE WALL—1927
Etching
4 x 3

92. A YOUTH—1928
Etching
6 x 4

93. AT THE BASE OF THE FLAGPOLE—1928
Etching
5 x 6

94. LOOKING OVER THE WALL—1928
Etching
5⅞ x 4

95. 14th STREET—1928
   Etching
   4⅞ x 10¾

96. MAN STANDING—1929
Etching
5⅞ x 4

97. UNION SQUARE MAN—1929
Etching
3⅞ x 2⅞

98. WAITING—1930
Etching
5⅞ x 4

99. SPECTATORS—1930
Etching
7 x 5

100. CONVERSATION—1931
Etching
6 x 4

101. READING THE NEWSPAPER—1931
Etching
6⅞ x 4⅞

102. LAUGHING GIRL—1934
Etching
4⅞ x 3⅞

103. THE NOON HOUR—1935
Etching
6⅞ x 4⅞
Edition of 40

104. SHOWING THE SNAPSHOT—1936
Etching
4 x 3

105. LAUGHING HEAD—1936
Etching
4¼ x 3¼
Edition of 30

106. GIRLS SITTING IN UNION SQUARE FOUNTAIN—1936
Etching
5⅞ x 4⅞

107. OFFICE GIRLS—1938
Etching
7⅞ x 4⅞
Edition of 50

108. LUNCH COUNTER—1940
Etching
7⅜ x 4

109. ENCOUNTER—1941
Etching
8⅛ x 5½
Edition of 40

110. THE COAT—1941
Etching
7½ x 4½

111. REACHING FOR COAT SLEEVE—1943
Etching
5⅞ x 4

112. CONVERSATION—1943
Engraving
6⅞ x 4⅞

113. PUTTING ON THE COAT (Front View)—1943
Etching
6 x 3⅞

114. DEPARTURE—1944
Etching
5½ x 3½

115. ICE CREAM CONES #1—1945
Etching
7½ x 4

116. ICE CREAM CONES #2—1945
Etching
7⅛ x 3½

117. TIDYING UP—1946
Etching
4 x 3

118. MAN TYING HIS SHOES—1946
Etching
4 x 3

119. MAN AT FOUNTAIN—1946
Etching
4⅝ x 3¼
Unique

120. MENDING—1947
Etching
4⅞ x 3

121. IN THE BUS—1947
Etching
4⅞ x 3⅛

122. DOUBLE DATE DELAYED—1948
Etching
5 x 3½

123. SUBWAY STATION UNDER UNION SQUARE—1948
Etching
12⅞ x 8⅞

124. GIRL WITH NEWSPAPER—1949
Etching
7⅜ x 4⅜

125. SODA FOUNTAIN—1950
Etching
7 x 5
Unique. Plate cut down to 6¼ x 4¼; now as "Outdoor Soda Fountain"
W.F. #676

126. STRAP HANGERS #2—1950
Etching
4⅞ x 3
Unique

127. 14th STREET ORIENTAL—1950
Etching
6 x 4

128. INTERLUDE—1952
Etching
7⅜ x 4⅜

129. TWO GIRLS OUTDOORS—1953
Etching
7½ x 4⅞

130. OUTDOOR SODA FOUNTAIN—1953
Etching
6¼ x 4¼
Plate of W. F. #36 "Soda Fountain"; cut down from 7 x 5

131. SUMMER TRAVELERS IN THE SUBWAY—1958
Etching
7½ x 4

132. SNACK BAR—1959
Etching
6⅞ x 4⅜

133. WALKING IN THE SUBWAY STATION—1961
Etching/Aquatint
6⅞ x 9¼
Miss Bishop's first aquatint

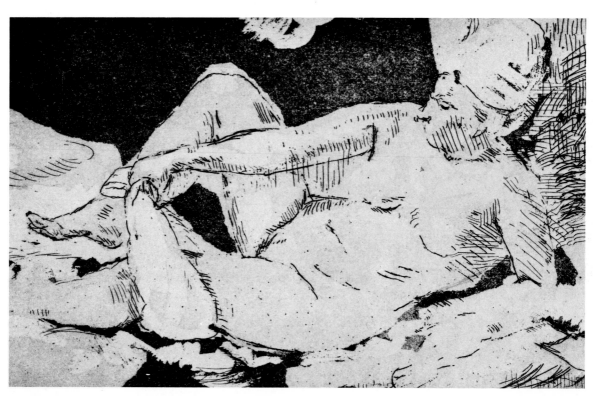

134. NUDE—1961
Etching/Aquatint
3½ x 6

135. NUDE—1963
Etching/Aquatint
5 x 7

136. WOMEN WALKING IN THE SUBWAY STATION—1963
Etching/Aquatint
8¾ x 6

137. IN THE SUBWAY—1963
Etching/Aquatint
9½ x 10¼
Also known as "Women Walking in the Subway Station #2"

138. LITTLE NUDE—1964
Etching/Aquatint
5¾ x 5

139. SUBWAY STATION UNDER GRAND CENTRAL—1966
Etching/Aquatint
8¾ x 15⅛
Artist's Proof—Edition of 30
Inscribed: For Lucille and Walter Fillin with Admiration and Love

140. THE COATS—1966
Etching/Aquatint
7½ x 7⅞
6/30

141. THREE WITH COATS—1967
Etching/Aquatint
7⅜ x 5½
15/35

142. TWO WITH COATS—1968
Etching/Aquatint
6⅞ x 4⅝
6/30

143. FIVE WOMEN WALKING—1969
Etching/Aquatint
7¾ x 9⅞
19/30

144. MEN AND WOMEN WALKING—1969
Etching/Aquatint
8⅜ x 11½
1/30

145. STUDENTS—1970
Etching/Aquatint
6⅞ x 4⅞
11/30

146. STUDENTS—1971
Etching/Aquatint
7¼ x 12⅞
7/35

147. CAMPUS STUDENTS—1972
Etching/Aquatint
8¼ x 14¼
1/30

148. STUDENT AND TWO GIRLS—1972
Etching/Aquatint
6⅞ x 5⅜
3/30

149. STUDENTS WITH BABY—1973
Etching/Aquatint
6⅞ x 4⅞
3/30

150. YOUNG PEOPLE—1974
Etching/Aquatint
6⅞ x 4⅞
4/30

151. SCHOOL GIRLS—1974
Etching/Aquatint
9¼ x 13
1/30

Catalogue

PAINTINGS

1. NUDE—n.d.
   Oil
   15 x 18
   Signed: Isabel Bishop, left corner
   National Academy of Design

2. PREOCCUPIED—n.d.
   Oil on Academy Board
   10⅝ x 12¾
   Not signed
   Wadsworth Atheneum, Bequest of
   Anne Parrish Titzell

3. STILL LIFE WITH BOTTLES—n.d.
   Oil
   18½ x 36½
   Signed: Isabel Bishop, lower right
   Wichita State University Collection
   Illus. No. 3

4. SELF-PORTRAIT—1927
   Oil
   14 x 13
   Not signed
   Leonore O. Miller
   Previous collection: Midtown Galleries
   Illus. No. 1

5. BOTTLES—1931
   Oil
   17 x 20
   Signed: Isabel Bishop, lower right
   Midtown Galleries
   Previous collection: The Artist
   Illus. No. 2

6. DANTE AND VIRGIL IN UNION
   SQUARE—1932
   Oil
   27 x 52
   Signed: Isabel Bishop, lower center
   Delaware Art Museum
   Previous collection: Midtown Galleries
   Exhibitions: Midtown Galleries, May
   3-28, 1960; Delaware Art Museum,
   "American Painting, 1840–1940,"
   January 7-February 6, 1972; Allentown
   Art Museum, "The City in American
   Painting," January 20-March 4, 1973
   Literature: *Art Students League News*,
   1971, Vol. 24, #5, reproduced; *Art
   News*, November 1971, p. 76, repro-
   duced, text p. 84; *Arts Magazine*,
   November 1971, p. 68; *Artforum*,
   January 1972, pp. 61–62, reproduced;
   Catalogue of "American Painting,
   1840–1940," Delaware Art Museum;
   Wilmington Evening Journal, De-
   cember 27, 1971, p. 49, reproduced
   Illus. No. 5

7. ON THE STREET (14th Street)—
   1932
   Oil
   14½ x 26
   Signed: Isabel Bishop, upper left
   Mr. and Mrs. Paul Wachs
   Previous collection: Midtown Galleries
   Exhibitions: "Paintings of the Thir-
   ties," Midtown Galleries, February
   5-March 2, 1974
   Illus. No. 6

8. UNION SQUARE—c. 1932
Oil
14 x 17⅜
Not signed
Nebraska Art Association, Nelle
Cochran Woods Collection
Previous collection: Midtown Galleries
Illus. No. 4

9. NUDE—1934
Oil on Composition Board
33 x 40
Signed: Isabel Bishop, lower center
Whitney Museum of American Art
Illus. No. 7

10. THE CLUB—1935
Oil and Tempera
20 x 24
Signed: Isabel Bishop, lower right
The Honorable and Mrs. J. Bertram
Wegman
Exhibitions: "Paintings of the Thirties," Midtown Galleries, February
5-March 2, 1974
Illus. No. 8

11. TWO GIRLS—1935*
Oil and Tempera on Press Wood
20 x 24
Signed: Isabel Bishop, lower left
The Metropolitan Museum of Art,
Arthur H. Hearn Fund, 1966

*At Whitney Museum of American Art only

12. STOOPING MAN—1936
Oil
12 x 10
Signed: Isabel Bishop, lower right
Mr. and Mrs. Joseph Walker
Illus. No. 9

13. HEAD OF A YOUNG WOMAN
—c. 1937
Oil and Tempera on Gesso Panel
20 x 17
Signed: Isabel Bishop, upper right
Mrs. C. Frederick Huntington

14. TIDYING UP—c. 1938
Oil on Masonite
15 x 11½
Signed: Bishop, upper left
Indianapolis Museum of Art, Delavan
Smith Fund Purchase
Previous collection: Midtown Galleries
Exhibitions: "Living American Painters," John Herron Art Museum,
January 24-February 28, 1943; "Celebrate Ohio," Akron Art Institute, September 27-November 7, 1971
Publications: *Art Bulletin*, June 1943,
pp. 14–15, illus., D. M. Mattison;
Catalogue of "Celebrate Ohio," Akron
Art Institute, 1971
Illus. No. 11

15. LAUGHING HEAD—1938
Oil
13 x 12
Signed: Isabel Bishop, lower right
The Butler Institute of American Art
Illus. No. 10

16. NUDE BY STREAM—1938
Oil and Tempera on Gesso Panel
25½ x 19¾
Not signed
Estate of William Benton

17. TWO GIRLS WITH A BOOK—1938
Oil and Tempera on Gesso Panel
20 x 24
Signed: Isabel Bishop, lower center
Mrs. W. Leicester van Leer
Previous collection: Midtown Galleries
Exhibitions: Cincinnati Art Museum,
1938; Worcester Museum of Art;
Zintag-Newport Show, 1938; Whitney
Museum, 1938; Carnegie Institute,
"Survey of American Painting, 1940"
Publications: Midtown Galleries
catalogue, 1939, reproduced; *Art
Digest*, February 1939, reproduced;
Parnassus Magazine, February 1939,
reproduced
Illus. No. 13

18. WAITING—1938
Oil and Tempera on Gesso Panel
29 x 22½
Signed: Isabel Bishop, upper right
The Newark Museum
Previous collection: Midtown Galleries
Exhibitions: Canadian Circuit Exhibi-
tion, 1939–40; San Francisco Golden
Gate Exhibition, 1939; Chicago Art In-
stitute; Fort Dodge Federation of Arts
Exhibition; Art Week Exhibition, 1941;
National Academy of Design, Detroit
Institute of Art; American Academy of
Arts and Letters Annual Exhibition,
1943; Brooklyn Museum Exhibitions,
1951; The American Federation of
Arts, "Mother and Child in Modern
Art," August 1964; Midtown Galleries,
"The Thirties," 1973
Publications: *Magazine of Art*, March
1939, reproduced; *Who* Magazine, Feb-
ruary 1942; Newark Museum Associa-
tion Catalogue of Paintings, 1944;
*Revolution and Tradition in Modern
American Art*, 1951; Monograph on
Isabel Bishop by Karl Lunde, 1971
Illus. No. 12

19. OFFICE GIRLS—1939
Oil on Masonite
36 x 22
Signed: Isabel Bishop, lower left
Private collection
Exhibitions: Colby College
Illus. No. 14

20. AT THE NOON HOUR—1939
Tempera and Pencil on Composition
Board
25 x 18
Not signed
Museum of Fine Arts, Springfield,
Massachusetts
Illus. No. 16

21. LUNCH HOUR—1939
Oil on Panel
27 x 17½
Signed: Isabel Bishop, upper left
Mrs. Alan D. Gruskin
Exhibitions: "Artist for Victory,"

1942–43; Albright Museum, Buffalo, New York, February 1943; Detroit Art Institute, April 1942; American Academy of Arts and Letters, May 1943; Oberlin College, April 1947; One Man Show, Midtown Galleries, May 1949; Virginia Museum of Fine Arts, 1961; "The New York Painter, A Century of Teaching," Marlboro-Gerson Gallery, August 26-October 14, 1967; "The Image in 20th Century America," Heckscher Museum, August 13-October 27, 1968; Amherst College, March 1969; New Jersey State Museum, Trenton, May 2-July 5, 1970; Akron Art Institute's "Celebrate Ohio," September 27-November 7, 1971; Midtown Galleries, "Paintings of the Thirties," February 5-March 2, 1974; "In Her Own Image," Samuel S. Fleisher Art Memorial, Philadelphia, April 4-May 14, 1974
Publications: *Art Digest*, April 1, 1945
Illus. No. 15

22. RESPITE—1939
Oil and Tempera on Gesso Panel
18¾ x 15½
Signed: Isabel Bishop, lower left
Mrs. Louis Hausman
Exhibitions: One Man Show, Midtown Galleries, May 1949

23. ENCOUNTER—1940
Oil and Tempera
23¾ x 15¾
Signed: Isabel Bishop, lower left

St. Louis Art Museum, Eliza McMillan Fund
Exhibitions: "The 36th Annual Exhibition: Trends in American Painting Today," The City Art Museum of St. Louis, January 25-February 28, 1942, Cat. No. 2; "Group Exhibition of Paintings by American Artists," Detroit Institute of Arts, April 13-May 10, 1943, Cat. No. 1
Illus. No. 17

24. ENCOUNTER #2—1940
Oil
24 x 16
Not signed
Richard and Bruce Gelb

25. HEAD #3—c. 1940–47
Oil on Masonite
16 x 11
Signed: Isabel Bishop, upper right
The Florida Gulf Coast Art Center
Exhibitions: Retrospective Group Show, Midtown Galleries, 1948; California Palace of the Legion of Honor, November 1948; One Man Show, Midtown Galleries, 1949; Des Moines Art Center, Special Group Oil Show, November 1950-January 1951; Midtown Summer Group, July 14-August 29, 1952; Southeastern Circuit, 1952-1953 Season; Florida Gulf Coast Art Center, Permanent Collection, acquired 1952

26. GIRL IN NEW YORK—c. 1941
Oil
20 x 16
Not signed
Colorado Springs Fine Arts Center
Previous collections: Midtown Galleries, The Artist
Exhibitions: Exhibition of Contemporary American Art, New York World's Fair, 1939; National Academy, 1940; Midwestern University, Wichita Falls, Kansas, 1951; Paintings from the Permanent Collection, Colorado Springs Fine Arts Center, 1965, 1966; "Colonial to Contemporary Art Through America," Colorado Springs Fine Arts Center, 1973–74

27. GIRL READING—1941
Oil
17 x 12
Signed: Isabel Bishop, lower right
Robert Cross Vergobbi

28. TAKING OFF HER COAT—c. 1941
Oil on Board
13⅞ x 8
Signed: Isabel Bishop, lower right
Dr. Martin H. Bush
Illus. No. 18

29. ICE CREAM CONES—1942
Oil and Tempera on Masonite
34 x 20
Not signed
Museum of Fine Arts, Boston, Charles Henry Hayden Fund

Previous collections: Midtown Galleries
Exhibitions: "Bishop," Midtown Galleries, 1949, No. 8; "Ten Women Who Paint," Smith College Museum, 1949, No. 1
Illus. No. 19

30. RESTING—1943
Oil on Gesso Panel
16 x 17
Signed: Isabel Bishop, upper right
Dr. and Mrs. Howard C. Taylor, Jr.
Illus. No. 21

31. SMALL NUDE—1943
Oil on Gesso Panel
15 x 13¾
Not signed
Theresa Shirer

32. STRAP HANGERS—c. 1943
Oil and Tempera on Gesso Panel
20 x 16
Not signed
Lawrence Arine
Previous collection: Cranbrook Academy of Art
Exhibitions: Grand Rapids Art Museum
Illus. No. 20

33. TWO GIRLS OUTDOORS—1944
Oil
30 x 18
Signed: Isabel Bishop, lower right
The Corcoran Gallery of Art
Illus. No. 22

34. FRIENDS—c. 1945
Oil on Panel
17 x 11¼
Signed: Isabel Bishop, lower right
Chauncey L. Waddell
Exhibitions: Pennsylvania Academy of Fine Arts, 1946; San Francisco Midtown Galleries, October 1946; Houston Museum of Fine Arts, January 1949; One Man Show, Midtown Galleries, May 1949; Florida Coast Circuit, 1949–1950; Cushman Gallery, Houston, Texas, January 1957; Berkshire Museum, August, 1957

35. MENDING—1945
Oil on Composition Board
25 x 16½
Signed: Isabel Bishop, lower left
Sara Roby Foundation, New York
Previous collection: The Artist
Exhibitions: Carnegie Institute, 1945; Pepsi-Cola Annual, 1946; California Palace of the Legion of Honor, 1947; Virginia Museum, 1948, 1950; Audubon Artists, 1952; John Herron Art Institute, 1953; Kenneth Hayes Miller Memorial Show, 1953; Munson-Williams-Proctor Institute, 1953; National Academy of Design, 1953; Butler Art Institute, 1953; Ogunquit Museum of Art, 1954; Century Club, New York, 1954; Third Biennial of American Painting, 1955; The Collection of the Sara Roby Foundation at the Whitney Museum of American Art, April 29-June 14, 1959 and then circulated by the museum throughout the United States until March, 1962; South American tour—United States Information Agency, May 1962-July 1963; The Collection of the Sara Roby Foundation—circulated throughout the United States and Canada under the auspices of The American Federation of Arts, New York, from September 1966-December 1970; Main Street Gallery, Nantucket, May 1972; "Americans: Individualists at Work," circulated throughout the United States and Canada under the auspices of The American Federation of Arts, New York, from September 1972-September 1974
Publications: The Collection of the Sara Roby Foundation, April 29-June 14, 1959, Whitney Museum of American Art
Illus. No. 23

36. GIRL READING NEWSPAPER—1946
Oil
29 x 18
Not signed
Nelson Gallery-Atkins Museum, Bequest of Marie P. McCune
Exhibitions: "Painting in the United States, 1946," Carnegie Institute, October 10-December 8, 1946; "Paintings

197

by Isabel Bishop, Sculpture by
Dorothea Greenbaum," New Jersey
State Museum, May 2-July 5, 1970
Publications: "Painting in the United
States," 1946 Catalogue; "Paintings by
Isabel Bishop, Sculpture by Dorothea
Greenbaum," Cat. No. 10, reproduced
Pl. No. 10
Illus. No. 24

37. NUDE IN INTERIOR—1947
Oil and Tempera
21 x 18
Not signed
The New Britain Museum of American
Art, Stephen Lawrence Fund
Illus. No. 25

38. DOUBLE DATE DELAYED—1948
Oil on Board
22⅛ x 18⅛
Not signed
Munson-Williams-Proctor Institute
Previous collection: Midtown Galleries
Exhibitions: Carnegie Institute, "Paint-
ing in the United States, 1948," Oc-
tober 14-December 12, 1948; Midtown
Galleries, "Selected American Paint-
ings 1900-1950," April 30-May 21,
1950; Albany Institute of History and
Art, "20th Century Moderns," Feb-
ruary 1-23, 1957; Akron Art Institute,
"Celebrate Ohio," September 25-
November 7, 1971
Illus. No. 26

39. NUDE BENDING—1949
Oil and Tempera
21 x 24
Not signed
Sara Mary B. Roby
Previous collection: The Artist
Exhibitions: One Man Show, Midtown
Galleries, May 1949; Carnegie Insti-
tute, October 13-December 11, 1949;
Pennsylvania Academy Oil Show,
January 22-February 26, 1950; Toledo
Museum Summer Show, 1950; Met-
ropolitan Museum of Art, American
Painting Show, December 9-February
25, 1951; National Academy Annual,
March 23-April 8, 1951; Midtown Gal-
leries, 25th Anniversary Show, May
7-June 8, 1957
Illus. No. 27

40. HOMEWARD—1951
Oil and Tempera
26 x 20
Not signed
Mr. and Mrs. Stanley J. Wolf
Exhibitions: Midtown Galleries Ret-
rospective, 1951; Midtown Galleries,
Midtown Group, 1951; Worcester Art
Museum, November 6-December 14,
1952; Midtown Galleries, "Bishop—
Paintings and Drawings," October
25-November 19, 1955
Publications: *Art News*, November
1951, "Bishop Paints a Picture,"
Dorothy Seckler, reproduced in color
Illus. No. 28

41. GIRLS IN THE SUBWAY
STATION—1953
Oil and Tempera on Gesso Panel
32 x 20
Not signed
Dr. Beatrice B. Berle
Illus. No. 30

42. INTERLUDE—1953
Oil and Tempera on Gesso Panel
34 x 20
Signed: Isabel Bishop, lower left
Mr. and Mrs. Alexander D. Falck, Jr.
Previous collection: Midtown Galleries;
The Artist
Illus. No. 29

43. SNACK BAR—c. 1954
Oil on Panel
13½ x 11⅛
Not signed
Columbus Gallery of Fine Arts, Howald
Fund Purchase
Previous collection: Midtown Galleries
Illus. No. 31

44. PAUSE TO REFRESH—1955
Oil and Tempera on Gesso Panel
30½ x 16⅛
Not signed
Mrs. Louise Miller Smith
Illus. No. 32

45. SUBWAY—1956
Oil and Tempera
25 x 18
Not signed
Barbara and Stuart Bartle

46. THE BATHER—c. 1955
Tempera
18 x 21
Not signed
University of Arizona Museum of Art
C. Leonard Pfeiffer Collection
Publications: Catalogue of the C.
Leonard Pfeiffer Collection, University
of Arizona Museum of Art, Cat. No. 6
Illus. No. 33

47. SUBWAY READING—1956
Oil
24½ x 17¾
Not signed
Private collection
Illus. No. 34

48. SUBWAY SCENE—1957-58
Tempera and Oil on Gesso Panel
40 x 28
Not signed
Whitney Museum of American Art
Illus. No. 35

49. UNDRESSING—1959
Oil
33 x 29½
Not signed
Atlanta University
Illus. No. 36

50. COKE BREAK—1960
Oil and Tempera on Board
29⅝ x 20½
Signed: Isabel Bishop, lower right
Tennessee Fine Arts Center, Gift of
Dr. and Mrs. Charles E. Wells

Previous collection: Dr. and Mrs. Charles E. Wells
Exhibitions: "Isabel Bishop—Exhibition of Paintings," Midtown Galleries, April 4-29, 1967
Illus. No. 40

51. SODA FOUNTAIN WITH PASSERS BY—1960
Oil and Tempera
24 x 36
Not signed
Virginia Museum of Fine Arts
Exhibitions: 30th Anniversary Loan Exhibition, Midtown Galleries, November 23-December 15, 1962; Anniversary Convocation, Mary Baldwin College, April 18-May 1, 1968; Newly Elected Members Exhibition, American Academy of Arts and Letters, May 17-June 18, 1972
Publications: *American Artist*, Ernest Harms, "The Art of Isabel Bishop," pp. 28-33, illus. p. 30
Illus. No. 41

52. STUDY FOR "SODA FOUNTAIN WITH PASSERS BY"—1960
Oil and Tempera
13¼ x 23
Not signed
Mr. and Mrs. Robert E. Blum
Illus. No. 37

53. STUDY FOR "UNDRESSING ON THE BED"—1960
Oil
19 x 38

Signed: Isabel Bishop, lower right
Midtown Galleries
Previous collection: The Artist
Exhibitions: Virginia Museum Traveling Exhibition, 1963-65; Krannert Art Museum, Champaign, Illinois, March 5-April 9, 1967; Skidmore College, Saratoga Springs, January 6-30, 1970; National Arts Club, February 2-8, 1970; "Two Artists Exhibition," New Jersey State Museum, Trenton, May 2- July 5, 1970; "Three Figurative Painters," Midtown Galleries, October 26-November 20, 1971; Bronx Council on the Arts, November 15-December 3, 1971; National Academy of Design Annual Exhibition, February 24-March 19, 1972; Audubon Artists Annual Exhibition, January 17-February 3, 1974; "In Her Own Image," Samuel S. Fleisher Art Memorial, Philadelphia, April 4-May 14, 1974
Publications: Monograph on Isabel Bishop to be published by Harry N. Abrams, reproduced
Illus. No. 39

54. UNDRESSING ON THE BED—1960
Oil and Tempera on Gesso Panel
18½ x 37
Signed: Isabel Bishop, lower right
Mrs. William H. Kearns
Exhibitions: Virginia Museum of Fine Arts, 1961
Illus. No. 38

55. WOMAN UNDRESSING—1961
Oil and Tempera on Masonite

20¼ x 34
Signed: Isabel Bishop, lower right
Sue and David Workman
Illus. No. 42

56. WALKING IN THE SUBWAY
STATION—1963
Oil and Tempera
24 x 33
Not signed
Dr. and Mrs. Bronson S. Ray
Previous collection: Midtown Galleries
Illus. No. 44

57. WOMEN WALKING #2—1963
Oil and Tempera
27½ x 30½
Signed: Isabel Bishop, lower right
Dr. and Mrs. J. Robert Buchanan
Previous collection: Midtown Galleries
Illus. No. 43

58. NUDE REACHING—1964
Oil and Tempera
28 x 35
Signed: Isabel Bishop, lower right
National Academy of Design, Henry
Ward Ranger Fund
Previous collection: Midtown Galleries
Illus. No. 47

59. PREPARATION—1964
Oil and Tempera
22 x 20
Signed: Isabel Bishop, lower left
The William Benton Museum of Art,
The University of Connecticut, on loan
from the Estate of William Benton
Illus. No. 45

60. LITTLE NUDE—1964
Oil
26½ x 21¼
Signed: Isabel Bishop, lower right
Sue and David Workman
Illus. No. 46

61. STUDY FOR "DRINKING
FOUNTAIN"—1965
Oil
15 x 12
Signed: Isabel Bishop, lower right
Wake Forest University College Union
Collection of Contemporary Art
Illus. No. 48

62. GETTING DRESSED—1966
Oil and Tempera on Gesso Panel
22 x 20
Signed: Isabel Bishop, lower left
Dr. and Mrs. Howard C. Taylor, Jr.
Illus. No. 49

63. FIVE WOMEN WALKING #1—1967
Oil and Tempera on Gesso Panel
31½ x 39½
Not signed
Private collection
Previous collection: The Artist
Exhibitions: "35th Anniversary Exhibi-
tion 'Report,'" Midtown Galleries,
March 14-April 1, 1967; Isabel Bishop
Show, Midtown Galleries, April 4-April
29, 1967
Publications: Reproduced in Bishop
Catalogue of April 1967
Illus. No. 51

64. FIVE WOMEN WALKING #2
—c. 1967
Oil on Board
32 x 40
Signed: Isabel Bishop, lower right
Wichita State University Collection
Illus. No. 53

65. SEATED NUDE—1967
Oil and Tempera on Gesso Panel
23 x 21
Signed: Isabel Bishop, lower right
center
Mr. and Mrs. John R. Wierdsma
Previous collections: Mr. and Mrs.
Nathan Allen; Midtown Galleries
Illus. No. 54

66. STUDY FOR "THE COATS"—1967
Oil and Tempera on Gesso Panel
28 x 30
Not signed
Mrs. Louise Miller Smith
Illus. No. 52

67. STUDENTS WALKING—1967
Oil and Tempera
31½ x 48
Signed: Isabel Bishop, lower right
Mr. and Mrs. Henry A. Ashforth, Jr.
Illus. No. 50

68. STUDENTS WALKING #2—1968
Oil and Tempera
31½ x 48
Signed: Isabel Bishop, lower right
Midtown Galleries
Previous collection: The Artist

Exhibitions: "39th Anniversary Exhibition," Midtown Galleries, February 16-March 13, 1971; "Highlights of the Season," Midtown Galleries, June 26-July 27, 1973; "Summer Group Exhibition," Midtown Galleries, July 31-September 8, 1973; "Ranger Fund Exhibition," National Academy of Design, September 17-October 6, 1973; "Woman's Work—American Art '74," Civic Center Museum, Philadelphia, April 27-May 26, 1974
Illus. No. 55

69. SUBWAY STATION UNDER GRAND CENTRAL #2—1968
Oil on Gesso Panel
27 x 46
Signed: Isabel Bishop, lower right
Richard Shields
Previous collection: Midtown Galleries
Illus. No. 56

70. STREET SCENE—1969
Oil and Tempera
16½ x 23
Not signed
Richard Shields
Previous collection: Midtown Galleries
Exhibitions: Midtown Galleries Group Exhibitions, Fall 1970
Illus. No. 57

71. MEN AND GIRLS WALKING
—c. 1970
Oil on Masonite
28½ x 39½
Not signed

Mount Holyoke College Art Museum
Exhibitions: New Jersey State Museum, May 2-July 5, 1970; National Academy of Design, February 25-March 21, 1971; Midtown Galleries, October 26-November 20, 1971; Butler Institute of American Art, July 2-September 4, 1972; National Institute of Arts and Letters, Members' Exhibition, November 10-December 17, 1972
Illus. No. 58

72. STUDENTS—1971
Oil
29 x 40
Not signed
Sara Mary B. Roby
Previous collection: The Artist
Exhibitions: "Three Figurative Painters," October 26-November 20, 1971; American Academy of Arts and Letters, May 17-June 18, 1972; National Arts Club Members' Exhibit, January 12-28, 1973, (Best of Show Award for Oil)
Illus. No. 59

73. YOUNG GIRLS—1971
Oil and Tempera on Gesso Panel
26 x 39½
Not signed
A. Petcavage

74. CAMPUS STUDENTS #2—1972
Oil and Tempera
34 x 38½
Not signed
Mr. and Mrs. Joseph L. Braun

Previous collection: Midtown Galleries
Illus. No. 60

75. HIGH SCHOOL STUDENTS—1973
Oil
25 x 40
Not signed
Midtown Galleries
Previous collection: The Artist
Exhibitions: "149th Annual Exhibition," National Academy of Design, New York, February 23-March 16, 1974; "Highlights of the Season," Midtown Galleries, April 30-May 25, 1974; "Summer Group Exhibition," Midtown Galleries, June 24-July 26, 1974
Illus. No. 61

76. DRINKING FOUNTAIN—n.d.
Ink
3¼ x 3
Signed: I.B., lower right
The Fort Wayne Museum of Art
Previous collection: Midtown Galleries

77. GIRL WITH A COAT #1—n.d.
Ink
6⅜ x 3½
Signed: Lower left
Mrs. L. B. Wescott
Exhibitions: Summit Art Center, New Jersey, April 1974

78. GIRL WITH A COAT #2—n.d.
Ink Wash
6⅛ x 4
Signed: Lower left
Mrs. L. B. Wescott

Exhibitions: Summit Art Center, New Jersey, April 1974

79. MAN WALKING WITH SHOULDER BAG—n.d.
Drawing
7 x 4
Signed: Isabel Bishop, upper left
Whitney F. Hoyt

80. MAN WITH JACKET—n.d.
Ink Wash
5⅝ x 3⅞
Signed: Lower right
Mrs. L. B. Wescott
Exhibitions: Summit Art Center, New Jersey, April 1974

81. MEN SEATED—n.d.
Pen and Ink over Pencil
4½ x 3⅜
Signed: Isabel Bishop, lower right
Fogg Art Museum, Harvard University, Gift of Alan D. Gruskin of Midtown Galleries

82. MEN SEATED—n.d.
Pen and Ink over Pencil
6½ x 3⅓
Signed: Isabel Bishop, lower right
Fogg Art Museum, Harvard University, Gift of Alan D. Gruskin of Midtown Galleries

83. STUDY FOR "THE SUBWAY"—n.d.
Ink Wash
14⅝ x 23⅛
Not signed
Dr. and Mrs. Howard C. Taylor, Jr.

84. NUDE TOUCHING HER TOES —n.d.
Drawing
6¾ x 4¾
Signed: Isabel Bishop, lower right
Whitney F. Hoyt

85. NUDE WITH TOWEL—n.d.
Pen and Wash
4⅝ x 6⅝
Signed: Isabel Bishop, upper right
Mulvane Art Center of Topeka

86. TWO GIRLS OUTDOORS (Sketch for Painting)—n.d.
Pen and Wash
10¼ x 10¼
Signed: Isabel Bishop, upper right
The Corcoran Gallery of Art

87. WAITING—n.d.
Pen and Wash
5½ x 4⅛
Signed: Isabel Bishop, lower left
Dallas Museum of Fine Arts
Mrs. Edwin B. Hopkins Fund

88. WOMAN SEATED FACING LEFT (Study for Soda Fountain)—n.d.
Pen and Ink
11⅞ x 8½
Signed: Isabel Bishop, lower left
The Brooklyn Museum, Dick S. Ramsay Fund
Illus. No. 62

89. WOMAN SEATED FACING RIGHT
(Study for Soda Fountain)—n.d.
Pen and Ink
11⅜ x 7⅜
Signed: Isabel Bishop, lower left
The Brooklyn Museum, Dick S. Ramsay Fund
Illus. No. 63

90. UNTITLED—n.d.*
Pencil
8 x 5¾ (sight)
Signed: Isabel Bishop, lower right
Dorothy Reich
*At the University of Arizona Museum of Art only.

91. STUDY FOR "THE BOOTBLACK"
—c. 1931-32
Watercolor
19⅜ x 16½
Signed: Isabel Bishop, lower right
Weatherspoon Art Gallery, Dillard Collection Purchase, 1972
University of North Carolina at Greensboro
Previous collections: Midtown Galleries; The Artist
Illus. No. 64

92. VIRGIL AND DANTE IN UNION
SQUARE—1932
Pencil Drawing
13 x 26
Not signed
Pennsylvania State University
Illus. No. 65

93. TWO GIRLS, STUDY—1934
Ink
9¼ x 6
Signed: Isabel Bishop, lower left
Susan and Herbert Adler
Illus. No. 66

94. STUDY FOR "THE CLUB"—1935
Wash, Chalk, Pencil and Oil
16½ x 19¾
Signed: Isabel Bishop, lower right
Edward Jacobson
Illus. No. 67

95. WAITING—1935
Pen, Ink and Wash
7⅛ x 6
Signed: Isabel Bishop, lower right
Whitney Museum of American Art
Illus. No. 68

96. IN THE PARK—c. 1935-37
Ink
6 x 4⅜
Signed: Isabel Bishop, lower left
American Academy of Arts and Letters
Previous collection: The Artist

97. TWO GIRLS—c. 1935
Ink and Wash
4½ x 6
Signed: Isabel Bishop, lower right
Michael M. Wachs

98. TWO MEN #2—c. 1935-57
Ink and Wash
4¾ x 3¾
Signed: I.B., lower right

American Academy of Arts and Letters
Previous collection: The Artist

99. ROSALYND—1936
Ink and Wash
4 x 3
Signed: Isabel Bishop, lower left
Susan and Herbert Adler
Illus. No. 69

100. THE DAY'S NEWS—c. 1936
Ink
5¼ x 4
Signed: Isabel Bishop, lower right
Michael M. Wachs
Illus. No. 70

101. NUDE SEATED—1938
Ink Wash
5⅞ x 6⅝
Signed: Isabel Bishop, lower left
Edward Jacobson
Illus. No. 71

102. CARD GAME—1942
Watercolor
17⅞ x 18⅞
Not signed
The Brooklyn Museum, Henry L. Batterman Fund
Previous collections: Midtown Galleries; The Artist
Exhibitions: The Brooklyn Museum, "International Watercolor Exhibition—Twelfth Biennial," April 9-May 23, 1943, Cat. No. 10; The Art Institute of Chicago, "55th Annual American Exhibition: Watercolors and Drawings," June 8-August 20, 1944, Cat. No. 74
References: Note on the subject of the watercolor in letter from the artist to John I. H. Baur, Curator, dated May 20, 1943: "The picture has to do with a scene I often used to sketch while waiting for the 7:51 train from Riverdale station, in the morning. Workers on the railroad gathered here (last year, that is, for there is no longer any work done on the railroad). They played cards on the tool box while waiting for the foreman, and 8:00 to come."
Illus. No. 74

103. ICE CREAM CONES—c. 1938-39
Pen and Ink Wash
8 x 5
Signed: I. Bishop, lower left
Susan and Herbert Adler
Illus. No. 72

104. ICE CREAM CONES—1940
Pencil with White Crayon
35¾ x 21½
Not signed
St. Lawrence University,
Gift of Charles Z. Offin Art Fund, Inc.
Previous collection: Midtown Galleries
Exhibitions: "A Selection of Drawings and Prints 1932-1973," Midtown Galleries, January 8-February 2, 1974; "Paintings by Isabel Bishop, Sculpture by Dorothea Greenbaum," New Jersey

State Museum, Trenton, May 2-July 5, 1970
Publications: "Paintings by Isabel Bishop, Sculpture by Dorothea Greenbaum," Cat. No. 38
Illus. No. 75

105. TWO GIRLS—c. 1941
Gouache Drawing
17 x 23
Not signed
The Butler Institute of American Art
Illus. No. 73

106. SUBWAY RIDERS—1944
Ink
5⅞ x 4⅛
Signed: Isabel Bishop, lower right front
The Charles R. Penney Collection
Publications: To be included in the forthcoming book: *Isabel Bishop*, by Karl Lunde, published by Harry N. Abrams, Inc.

107. MAKE-UP—c. 1945
Ink, Wash
8 x 5
Signed: Isabel Bishop, lower right
Addison Gallery of American Art, Phillips Academy, Andover, Massachusetts

108. SEATED NUDE—c. 1945
Ink and Wash
7 x 6½
Signed: Isabel Bishop, lower left
Los Angeles County Museum of Art,

Gift of Miss Bella Mabury for the Paul Rodman Mabury Collection
Exhibitions: First Biennial Exhibition of Drawings by American Artists, Cat. No. 44, Los Angeles County Museum, 1945; Chouinard Art Institute, Los Angeles, 1952
Illus. No. 76

109. MENDING—c. 1947
Pen and Ink
9 x 6
Signed: Isabel Bishop, lower left
Mr. and Mrs. Floyd T. Amsden

110. STUDY FOR "COKE BREAK"-A
—c. 1960
Pen and Ink
7½ x 4⅛
Signed: Isabel Bishop, lower left
The Tennessee Botanical Gardens and Fine Arts Center
Gift of the artist
Illus. No. 78

111. STUDY FOR "COKE BREAK"-B
—c. 1960
Pen and Ink
7½ x 4⅛
Signed: Isabel Bishop, lower right
The Tennessee Botanical Gardens and Fine Arts Center
Gift of the artist
Illus. No. 79

112. STUDY FOR "COKE BREAK"-C
—c. 1960

Pen and Ink
7½ x 4½
Signed: Isabel Bishop, lower left
The Tennessee Botanical Gardens and
Fine Arts Center
Gift of the artist
Illus. No. 80

113. STUDY FOR "COKE BREAK"-D
—c. 1960
Pen and Ink
6¾ x 4½
Signed: Isabel Bishop, lower right
The Tennessee Botanical Gardens and
Fine Arts Center
Gift of the artist
Illus. No. 81

114. STUDY FOR "COKE BREAK"-E
—c. 1960
Pen and Ink
7 x 4½
Signed: Isabel Bishop, lower left
The Tennessee Botanical Gardens and
Fine Arts Center
Gift of the artist
Illus. No. 82

115. STUDY FOR "COKE BREAK"-F
—c. 1960
Pen and Ink
6¾ x 4½
Signed: Isabel Bishop, lower right
The Tennessee Botanical Gardens and
Fine Arts Center
Gift of the artist
Illus. No. 83

116. STUDY FOR "COKE BREAK"-G
—c. 1960
Pen and Ink
6¼ x 3¾
Signed: Isabel Bishop, lower right
The Tennessee Botanical Gardens and
Fine Arts Center
Gift of the artist
Illus. No. 84

117. STUDY FOR "COKE BREAK"-H
—c. 1960
Pen and Ink
5½ x 4¼
Signed: Isabel Bishop, lower right
The Tennessee Botanical Gardens and
Fine Arts Center
Gift of the artist
Illus. No. 85

118. STUDY FOR "COKE BREAK"-I
—c. 1960
Pen and Ink
6¼ x 3¼
Signed: Isabel Bishop, lower left
The Tennessee Botanical Gardens and
Fine Arts Center
Gift of the artist
Illus. No. 86

119. GIRL TAKING OFF SWEATER
—1970
Ink, Wash
6½ x 4½
Signed: Isabel Bishop, lower left
Mr. and Mrs. William S. Mills
Illus. No. 77

All etchings and aquatints are from the collection of Mr. and Mrs. Walter Fillin.

120. IN FRONT OF 42nd STREET
LIBRARY—1925
Etching
3 x 4
Illus. No. 89

121. NUDE—1925
Etching
6½ x 5⅝
Illus. No. 87

122. NUDE—1925
Etching
10 x 6¾
Inscribed: To Walter Fillin with Warm
Greetings
Illus. No. 88

123. LEANING ON THE WALL—1927
Etching
4 x 3
Illus. No. 91

124. OVER THE WALL—1927
Etching
2½ x 3½
Illus. No. 90

125. A YOUTH—1928
Etching
6 x 4
Illus. No. 92

126. AT THE BASE OF THE FLAG-
POLE—1928
Etching
5 x 6
Illus. No. 93

127. 14th STREET—1928
Etching
4⅞ x 10¾
Illus. No. 95

128. LOOKING OVER THE WALL—1928
Etching
5⅞ x 4
Illus. No. 94

129. MAN STANDING—1929
Etching
5⅞ x 4
Illus. No. 96

130. UNION SQUARE MAN—1929
Etching
3⅞ x 2⅞
Illus. No. 97

131. SPECTATORS—1930
Etching
7 x 5
Illus. No. 99

132. WAITING—1930
Etching
5⅞ x 4
Illus. No. 98

133. CONVERSATION—1931
Etching
6 x 4
Illus. No. 100

134. READING THE NEWSPAPER
—1931
Etching
6⅞ x 4⅞
Illus. No. 101

135. LAUGHING GIRL—1934
Etching
4⅞ x 3⅞
Illus. No. 102

136. THE NOON HOUR—1935
Etching
6⅞ x 4⅞
Edition of 40
Illus. No. 103

137. GIRLS SITTING IN UNION
SQUARE FOUNTAIN—1936
Etching
5⅞ x 4⅞
Illus. No. 106

138. LAUGHING HEAD—1936
Etching
4¼ x 3¼
Edition of 30
Illus. No. 105

139. SHOWING THE SNAPSHOT—1936
Etching
4 x 3
Illus. No. 104

140. OFFICE GIRLS—1938
Etching
7⅞ x 4⅞
Edition of 50
Illus. No. 107

141. LUNCH COUNTER—1940
Etching
7⅜ x 4
Illus. No. 108

142. ENCOUNTER—1941
Etching
8⅛ x 5½
Edition of 40
Illus. No. 109

143. THE COAT—1941
Etching
7½ x 4½
Illus. No. 110

144. CONVERSATION—1943
Engraving
6⅞ x 4⅞
Illus. No. 112

145. PUTTING ON THE COAT
(Front View)—1943
Etching
6 x 3⅞
Illus. No. 113

146. REACHING FOR COAT SLEEVE
—1943
Etching
5⅞ x 4
Illus. No. 111

147. DEPARTURE—1944
Etching
5½ x 3½
Illus. No. 114

148. ICE CREAM CONES #1—1945
Etching
7½ x 4
Illus. No. 115

149. ICE CREAM CONES #2—1945
Etching
7⅛ x 3½
Illus. No. 116

150. MAN AT FOUNTAIN—1946
Etching
4⅝ x 3 ¼
Unique
Illus. No. 119

151. MAN TYING HIS SHOES—1946
Etching
4 x 3
Illus. No. 118

152. TIDYING UP—1946
Etching
4 x 3
Illus. No. 117

153. IN THE BUS—1947
Etching
4⅞ x 3⅛
Illus. No. 121

154. MENDING—1947
Etching
4⅞ x 3
Illus. No. 120

155. DOUBLE DATE DELAYED—1948
Etching
5 x 3½
Illus No. 122

156. SUBWAY STATION—1948
Etching
12⅞ x 8⅞
Illus. No. 123

157. GIRL WITH NEWSPAPER—1949
Etching
7⅜ x 4⅜
Illus. No. 124

158. 14th STREET ORIENTAL—1950
Etching
6 x 4
Illus. No. 127

159. SODA FOUNTAIN—1950
Etching
7 x 5
Unique. Plate cut down to 6¼ x 4¼, now
as "Outdoor Soda Fountain." W.F. #676
Illus. No. 125

160. STRAP HANGERS #2—1950
Etching
4⅞ x 3
Unique
Illus. No. 126

161. INTERLUDE—1952
Etching
7⅜ x 4⅜
Illus. No. 128

162. OUTDOOR SODA FOUNTAIN
—1953
Etching
6¼ x 4¼
Plate of W.F. #36 "Soda Fountain," cut
down from 7 x 5
Illus. No. 130

163. TWO GIRLS OUTDOORS—1953
Etching
7½ x 4⅞
Illus. No. 129

164. SUMMER TRAVELERS IN THE
SUBWAY—1958
Etching
7½ x 4
Illus. No. 131

165. SNACK BAR—1959
Etching
6⅞ x 4⅜
Illus. No. 132

166. NUDE—1961
Etching/Aquatint
3½ x 6
Illus. No. 134

167. WALKING IN THE SUBWAY
STATION—1961
Etching/Aquatint
6⅞ x 9¼
Miss Bishop's first aquatint
Illus. No. 133

168. IN THE SUBWAY—1963
Etching/Aquatint
9½ x 10¼
Also known as "Women Walking in the
Subway Station #2"
Illus. No. 137

169. NUDE—1963
Etching/Aquatint
5 x 7
Illus. No. 135

170. WOMEN WALKING IN THE
SUBWAY STATION—1963
Etching/Aquatint
8¾ x 6
Illus. No. 136

171. LITTLE NUDE—1964
Etching/Aquatint
5¾ x 5
Illus. No. 138

172. SUBWAY STATION UNDER
GRAND CENTRAL—1966
Etching/Aquatint
8¾ x 15⅛
Artist's Proof, Edition of 30.
Inscribed: For Lucille and Walter Fillin
with Admiration and Love
Illus. No. 139

173. THE COATS—1966
Etching/Aquatint
7½ x 7⅞
6/30
Illus. No. 140

174. THREE WITH COATS—1967
Etching/Aquatint
7⅜ x 5½
15/35
Illus. No. 141

175. TWO WITH COATS—1968
Etching/Aquatint
6⅞ x 4⅝
6/30
Illus. No. 142

176. FIVE WOMEN WALKING—1969
Etching/Aquatint
7¾ x 9⅞
19/30
Illus. No. 143

177. MEN AND WOMEN WALKING
—1969
Etching/Aquatint
8⅜ x 11½
1/30
Illus. No. 144

178. STUDENTS—1970
Etching/Aquatint
6⅞ x 4⅞
11/30
Illus. No. 145

179. STUDENTS—1971
Etching/Aquatint
7¼ x 12⅞
7/35
Illus. No. 146

180. CAMPUS STUDENTS—1972
Etching/Aquatint
8¼ x 14¼
1/30
Illus. No. 147

181. STUDENT AND TWO GIRLS—1972
Etching/Aquatint
6⅞ x 5⅜
3/30
Illus. No. 148

182. STUDENTS WITH BABY—1973
Etching/Aquatint
6⅞ x 4⅞
3/30
Illus. No. 149

183. SCHOOL GIRLS—1974
Etching/Aquatint
9¼ x 13
1/30
Illus. No. 151

184. YOUNG PEOPLE—1974
Etching/Aquatint
6⅞ x 4⅞
4/30
Illus. No. 150

Biography

1902 Born Cincinnati, Ohio. Daughter of Dr. J. Remsen Bishop, educator. Spent childhood in Detroit.

1918 Moved to New York City to study. Entered New York School of Applied Design for Women, to study illustration.

1920 Transferred to Art Students League of New York to study painting with Kenneth Hayes Miller and Guy Pène du Bois.

1926 Lived and worked in loft at 9 West 14th Street.

1932 Joined Midtown Galleries group.

1934 Married Dr. Harold G. Wolff, neurologist. Leased her Union Square studio.

1936 Appointed instructor at Art Students
–37 League.

1938 Commissioned by United States Government to paint mural at New Lexington, Ohio, Post Office.

1940 Son, Remsen N. Wolff, born. Elected Associate Member of National Academy of Design. Exhibited at New York World's Fair.

1941 Elected Academician of National Academy of Design. Studied engraving with Stanley William Hayter at New School for Social Research.

1944 Elected Member of National Institute of Arts and Letters.

1946 Elected Vice President of the National Institute of Arts and Letters. First woman officer since the Institute's founding in 1898.

1956 Taught at Skowhegan School of Paint-
–58 ing and Sculpture, Skowhegan, Maine.

1963 Resumed teaching at Skowhegan School (guest teacher and lecturer). Visiting artist, Yale University School of Fine Arts.

1964 Elected Benjamin Franklin Fellow, Royal Society of Arts, London.

1968 Awarded the National Arts Club Gold Medal of Honor.

1970 Continues to work at Union Square studio.

1974 Purchase Prize at the National Prints and Drawings at Mount Holyoke, Massachusetts.

Acknowledgments

This comprehensive Isabel Bishop retrospective exhibition, organized by The University of Arizona Museum of Art, owes its existence to the splendid cooperation between the Whitney Museum of American Art, Wichita State University, Brooks Memorial Art Gallery and The University of Arizona Museum of Art.

I have always admired Isabel Bishop's paintings—sensitive, authoritative, brilliant draughtsmanship, and a paint quality seldom equalled. When the opportunity presented itself to cooperate in an Isabel Bishop exhibition, I could not have been more pleased.

In talking with Tom Armstrong, Director of the Whitney Museum of American Art, I suggested that Dr. Sheldon Reich, Professor of Art History at the University of Arizona, do the main text. Dr. Martin Bush, Assistant Vice President for Academic Resources at Wichita State University, a friend of Isabel Bishop, volunteered additional material and John I. H. Baur, Director Emeritus of the Whitney Museum of American Art, a long-time friend, wrote the preface.

Funds from Wichita State University and Mr. Herbert S. Adler's generous contribution provided the means for Dr. Reich's trips to New York to personally interview and record on tape Isabel Bishop's memories of her career.

The University of Arizona Museum of Art's most grateful acknowledgment, as always, is directed toward the lenders, and especially Isabel Bishop herself, and Mrs. Alan D. Gruskin of the Midtown Galleries.

Lastly, it should be emphasized that a project as far-ranging and complex as the Isabel Bishop Retrospective can be undertaken only with a highly-trained and dedicated Museum Staff. Virtually every department of The University of Arizona Museum of Art participated in the exhibition and should receive full credit.

In lieu of expressions of thanks addressed to so many, I must mention here only Jeffrey Mitchell, my Assistant Director, for designing and supervising the publication of the catalogue: ISABEL BISHOP.

W. E. Steadman, Director
The University of Arizona Museum of Art

Bibliography

"Bishop's Progress," *Time*, XXXIII (Jan. 30, 1939), 36.

Breuning, Margaret, "Bishop Show Emphasizes Solidity," *Art Digest*, XXIII (May 1949), 15.

Campbell, Lawrence, "Isabel Bishop," *Art News*, LIV (Nov. 1955), 50.

de Kooning, Elaine, "Isabel Bishop," *Art News*, XLVII (May 1949), 46.

Canaday, John, "For Isabel Bishop: It's a Symbol of Endurance," *New York Times* (1967).

Dennison, George, "Isabel Bishop," *Arts*, XXXIV (May 1960), 58.

"Drawings by Isabel Bishop," *American Artist*, XIII (June 1949), 49–55.

Exhibition, Midtown Galleries, *Art Digest*, X (March 1, 1936), 16.

———, *Art Digest*, XIII (Feb. 1, 1939), 21.

———, *Art News*, XXXVII (Jan. 21, 1939), 11.

———, *Magazine of Art*, XXXII (Jan. 1939), 53.

———, *Art News*, XLI (June 1942), 42.

———, *Art News*, LIV (Nov. 1955), 50.

———, *Time*, LXVI (Nov. 28, 1955), 70.

———, *Art News*, LIX (May 1960), 14.

———, *Arts*, XXXIV (May 1960), 58.

"First Exhibition of Paintings in Ten Years, Midtown," *Studio*, CXXXVIII (Sept. 1949), 91.

"First Show Since 1949, Midtown," *Arts*, XXX (Nov. 1955), 50.

Harms, Ernest, "Light as the Beginning—The Art of Isabel Bishop," *American Artist*, XXV (Feb. 1961), 28-36, 60-62.

"Isabel Bishop Shows Her New York Types," *Art Digest*, X (Feb. 15, 1936), 19.

"Isabel Bishop to Hold One Man Show," *Art Digest*, VII (Oct. 1932), 13.

Johnson, Una E. and Jo Miller. *Isabel Bishop* (Monograph No. 2 in the series, American Graphic Artists of the Twentieth Century). Brooklyn, New York: The Brooklyn Museum, 1964.

Mattison, D. M., "Tidying Up by Bishop," John Herron Institute Bulletin, XXX (June 15, 1943), 14.

McBride, Henry, "Isabel Bishop," *New York Sun* (May 22, 1942).

"A Miller Pupil's Shackles Loosen," *Art Digest*, X (March 1, 1936), 16.

"Paintings and Drawings Shown at Midtown," *Art Digest*, XXIII (May 1, 1949), 15.

Pickett, G., "Twelve Women Painters of Distinction," *Independent Woman*, XXV (Nov. 1946), 348.

"Poet in the Square," *Time*, LXXV (May 16, 1960), 80 and 82.

Porter, Fairfield, "Art," *Nation*, CXC (May 21, 1960), 458.

Sawin, Martica, "Isabel Bishop," *Arts*, XXX (Nov. 1955), 50.

Sayre, A. H., "Substantial Technique in Isabel Bishop's Work," *Art News*, XXXIV (Feb. 22, 1936), 8.

Schuyler, James, "Isabel Bishop," *Art News*, LX (May 1960), 14.

Seckler, Dorothy, "Bishop Paints a Picture," *Art News*, L (Nov. 1951), 38–41+.

"Show at Midtown Gallery," *Art News*,
   LXVI (April 1967), 9.
Watson, Forbes, "Isabel Bishop," *Magazine
   of Art*, XXXII (Jan. 1939), 53–54.

WRITINGS BY ISABEL BISHOP

"Concerning Edges," *Magazine of Art*,
   XXXVIII (May 1945), 168–173.
"Drawing the Nude," *Art in America*, LI
   (Dec. 1963), 117.
"Isabel Bishop Discusses Genre Drawings,"
   American Artist, XVII (Summer 1953),
   46–47.
"Kenneth Hayes Miller," *Magazine of Art*,
   XLV (April 1952), 168–169.

Book design by Jeffrey Mitchell
Photography by Peter Balestrero
Typeset by Tucson Typographic Service
Printed by Isbell Printing Co.